MICHAEL PITTS

WHITAKER
HOUSE

HELP! I THINK GOD IS TRYING TO KILL ME

For speaking engagements, you may contact the author at:
Cornerstone Church
P. O Box 351690
Toledo, OH 43635
Web site: www.cornerstonetoledo.com

ISBN: 0-88368-774-7
Printed in the United States of America
© 2002 by M. A. P. S. Institute, Inc.

Whitaker House
30 Hunt Valley Circle
New Kensington, PA 15068
Visit our web site at: www.whitakerhouse.com

Library of Congress Cataloging-in-Publication Data pending

1 2 3 4 5 6 7 8 9 10 11 12 13 14 / 11 10 09 08 07 06 05 04 03 02

Contents

1
Sacred Suicide

1
Sacred Suicide

———◆◦◆◦◆———

"Your money or your life." We know what to do when a burglar makes this demand of us, but not when God does.
—Mignon McLaughlin

And they overcame him by the blood of the Lamb and by the word of their testimony, and they did not love their lives to the death.
—Revelation 12:11

$\mathcal{I}$'m going to do something unusual here—I'm going to begin this book with a prayer. Now, it may seem strange to you to begin a book with a prayer like many preachers do before beginning their sermons, but to me it's no different. You see, God has something He wants you to learn through the message in this book, and I have no desire to get in the way of it. I am no less concerned that I clearly communicate what God wants you to hear just because this is a book. I've learned over the years that prayer is the best way to focus on Him. And I believe that the Lord wants us to set our hearts and minds in a particular direction here, to see Him in a way that may be unusual or even uncomfortable for us, but it's, nevertheless, a way that will lead us to great truths about Him and His will concerning us. So let's pray.

> *Spirit of the Living God, touch every one whose eyes fall upon these pages. Make us understand what it means to live an uncommon and extraordinary life, to be the kind of person that we know You have called us to be. Help us to shake off the things that are holding us, the things that limit us, the things that tell us that we can't do or won't experience to fulfill Your calling. Let our faith rise up. Lord, our eyes are focused on You, the Alpha and Omega of all. Inhabit us and be glorified in Your habitation. In Jesus' Name. Amen.*

As a man or woman of God, you are called to live the uncommon life.

Friend, are you saved? If you are, then you, as a man or woman of God, are called to live the uncommon life. I don't mean just any uncommon life, in the way we would think of it—with great fame, fortune, or heroism. I'm talking about *the* uncommon life. There is only one kind— and that is the one that comes by accepting God's divine invitation to follow Him into eternity.

You may be thinking, *Oh, you mean the Christian life. That's not uncommon.* It should be. The life God has planned for you is not to look like everybody else's life. Your life should not follow the pattern of those who live in the world. People whose lives are touched by and directed by the Holy

Spirit stand out. They don't fit into the mold of common behavior or common belief. Holy Spirit-filled, full-of-the power-of-God mothers don't just bake cookies and look pretty. They know how to call on the Most High to deliver their children *before* they enter temptation. Power-filled men of God are more than just leaders. They are men of godly vision and valor. These men and women of God are *uncommon*. They don't waste their time seeking approval or validation because they've got a cloud and a pillar of fire leading them.

Not only do those who walk according to God's will for them live differently from the world's expectations, they also go *beyond* its expectations. Thus the uncommon life is also a life without worldly limits. It's normal for people who don't have a lot of money to become a little stingy about where it goes. It's uncommon for someone to give it anyway and find that it never runs out. It is common to gloat when your enemy falls into a pit, but it's uncommon to love him enough to help him out of it. It's not surprising when people become wealthy doing what they're good at. It's uncommon to prosper when their talent, intelligence, and influence fail. Uncommon people know that faith and favor succeed where ability and authority fall short!

Uncommon people know that faith and favor succeed where ability and authority fall short.

Deep down inside, you know that God has called you to something beyond "normal." It's one of those inherent, essential qualities of man that God has put inside our spirits. For example, you don't have to be taught to want to be free from oppression, whether that oppression comes from inside or outside influences. Just study the history of people groups throughout the world. Whenever one group or people was oppressed or dominated by another, they did anything and everything to be free! They might not have known that whom the Son sets free is really free, but there was something in them that said, "You're not going to hold me like this. I will fight against tyranny. I will fight against bondage."

In the same way, we know in our own hearts that we are to live an uncommon life. It's something God has put in us. Without a lot of teaching or theology, somehow we know that we are called to do more than just earn a paycheck. We know that we are called to do more than walk nonchalantly through life and, at the end, see what we have done. We know that, deep in our spirits, and for that reason many of us feel unfulfilled. We have this inward knowledge that our lives are supposed to be about something, but we can't figure out what that something is. If we can't figure it out, then our lives become meaningless.

We have an unquenchable thirst for something more.

So no matter what we have, whom we know, or what we have accomplished, there is an unquenchable thirst for something more. That thirst is for the uncommon life, the life God put us on this earth to live.

Characteristics of the Uncommon Life

Before we go much further, let me explain some things you need to know about living the uncommon life that will help you recognize it as it begins to develop in you. First of all, people who live the uncommon life do not have self as their focus. Unfortunately, too many people worship and serve themselves. That's their normal lifestyle. Everything in their lives is motivated and moved by their own wants and desires. Uncommon people, however, keep God's will as their focus, and therefore their lives are lived for purpose rather than possession. With every act and attitude, the uncommon man or woman declares his or her desire for God's kingdom to come and His will alone to be done.

Second, people who live an uncommon life use possessions to accomplish purpose. They do not see obtaining possessions as their purpose. Talent, wealth, prosperity, and influence become tools, not rewards, in the hands of a person who has chosen the uncommon life. In fact, God loves to bless people who will use those blessings to bless Him! He really doesn't care if you own things; He just doesn't want those things to possess you.

Third, the uncommon life is a life of giving and not taking. It is a life of service, not one in which you need to be served all the time. In short, the uncommon life is the life of a servant. Our flesh doesn't like this particular aspect, but it's true nonetheless. Make up your mind that if you want to do more for and in the kingdom of God, then you will have to hone your servanthood skills more, that you might be always ready and willing to do your Master's bidding.

Fourth, the uncommon life is a life of faith. It's a life unrestricted by circumstances and fear. It believes in the midst of contradictory, circumstantial evidence that something great really can happen. So many people today are pessimistic, including Christians. So many people feel "down" all the time. Why? They govern their lives by facts. They see the facts and come to conclusions that are only as great as the facts allow them to be. In other words, they end up right where they started! It is the uncommon person, however, who walks confidently ahead when the world screams at him to stop. It is the uncommon person who sits in peace while the world runs around in circles, frightened and confused. The person who lives the uncommon life doesn't draw his conclusions from the facts; he gets his from God, who has no limits and has no end!

Fifth, as is the case when you deal with an infinite, "omni-everything" God, the uncommon life is a life of miracles. Think about that for a minute. How do miracles happen? They can happen only when God is in control, not us. Miracles are not natural; they are supernatural. So to say that we are called to live uncommon lives is to say that we are to live miraculous lives. And that means we are to live lives that are out of our control.

An uncommon life is a life of miracles.

This is a stumbling block for many people. Most of us don't move out of an ordinary existence into a miraculous one because we don't want to let go of the reins. We don't want to let go of control. Our lives are securely managed, monitored, and manipulated by our own finite imaginations. We all say that we want miracles and that we want to live by faith, but the truth is we don't have room in our schedules for miracles. We set up our lives so that we can predict blessings rather than simply receive them. Living a miraculous life, living by faith, demands that we can't know everything that is going to happen.

Finally, God's power must reign in the uncommon life. If it doesn't, the best we can hope for is success according to human ability, expectation, and understanding. The Bible says that God has given us the same power that raised Jesus from the dead, but most of us either are too afraid to use it or have been satisfied with a counterfeit of it.

God's power, as it is described in Scripture, is translated from the Greek word *dunamis,* from which we get our English word *dynamite.* Think about a little stick of dynamite for a moment. Everything you need for an explosion is inside that stick, but in order for that power to be released, it has to be lit by a fire from another source. Without that fire, that stick of dynamite is only *potential* power. You might be able to hit somebody in the head with it, but that's about all the damage it will do. But, once that fire comes in contact with it...*Bam!*

We have to get out of the boat to walk with Jesus.

Just as in that stick of dynamite, the power that is in us is explosive! However, we can't control or direct such power; only God can. It is God who determines how far we go, how high we fly, and how many people we reach by the power of His "fire," the Holy Spirit. That's the way it is with the uncommon life. It is always greater than it appears to be. But, in order to live that life, we must be willing to relinquish control and believe that only God can direct us to that greatness. We have to let go and step out in faith or we will never live the uncommon and miraculous life. We have to get out of the boat to walk with Jesus; otherwise, we'll only run into disciples. Can you hear Him? He's calling you at this moment to come and walk with Him on the water!

A Matter of Life or Death

So, how do we find this uncommon life? Let's go to Mark chapter 8. There Jesus shows us the path we need to take.

> *When He had called the people to Himself, with His disciples also, He said to them, "Whoever desires to come after Me, let him deny himself, and take up his cross, and follow Me. For whoever desires to save his life will lose it, but whoever loses his life for my sake and the gospel's will save it. For what will it profit a man if he gains the whole world, and loses his own soul? Or what will a man give in exchange for his soul?"* (Mark 8:34–37)

I don't know if Jesus had as hard a time saying these words as preachers do preaching them. But I must say, I find it a lot easier to preach about these words than to hear them! And as hard as it is to hear them, it is even harder to live them. Nevertheless, these are the words of Christ Himself, and we must listen and take heed to them.

Do you remember the Scripture quoted at the beginning of this chapter? It says that the people of God overcome *"by the blood of the Lamb."* That refers to Jesus' blood, which was shed to atone for our sins. The verse then goes on to say that people also overcome by *"the word of their testimony."* Our testimony is our witness before the world. But, there is a third part that many Christians tend to overlook because it makes us uncomfortable: *"and they did not love their lives to the death."* The *Contemporary English Version* of the Bible says, *"They were willing to give up their lives"* (Rev. 12:11 CEV).

So, there you have it. The children of God, the victorious, the overcomers, the chosen few, the uncommon ones, are willing to give up their lives. This is what Jesus meant in Mark 8 when He told us to *"lose"* our lives. We have to be willing to give them up. In fact, Jesus went a step further. That word *"lose"* literally means to kill or destroy. Thus, in other words, Jesus expects us to kill or destroy our "life."(Obviously, I don't mean literal suicide, here. Keep reading!)

Sometimes you'll hear people read those verses in Mark 8 and they will say that a man has to "lose" his life in order to "find" it. That sounds sweet, but it's not entirely accurate. It gives the impression that you've just "temporarily misplaced" the life you live, and that someday you'll stumble upon it again. That image is misleading because it implies that the life we find will be the same life we lost. That's not what Jesus was saying. He doesn't expect us merely to set our lives aside while we follow Him; He expects us to destroy our lives *as they are* so that we will be able to follow Him without hindrance or distraction into the eternal life He promises us.

The uncommon ones are willing to give up their lives.

When you think about it, it's sort of like committing sacred suicide. In other words, you are voluntarily killing the type of person you used to be so that person you were called to be can live. Paul calls it "mortifying" the deeds and the members of the body (Rom. 8:13; Col. 3:5 KJV); "being conformed" to Christ's death (Phil. 3:10); and "reckoning yourself dead" to your old ways (Rom. 6:11). Romans 12:1 exhorts believers to *"present your bodies"* as living sacrifices. All of these passages indicate a choice on the part of the believer. The "death" is initiated and carried out by the individual believer as an act of his or her will. So in other words, God is telling us to voluntarily choose to become dead in order that Christ can live in us.

Some years ago a movie came out starring Sean Penn that was called *Dead Man Walking.* The actor played a prisoner on death row. The title came from the following tradition: Whenever a convicted man walked past the other cells on his way to be executed, the prison officials would solemnly call out, "Dead man walking!" Everyone who heard and saw that prisoner knew that despite the fact that he was living, breathing, walking, and sometimes crying and struggling, he was, for all intents and purposes, a dead man.

Choose to become dead so Christ can live in you.

People who live the uncommon life are "dead men walking." These men and women choose to become dead to worldly desires, drives, and directives. They're living, breathing, walking, and talking along with the rest of the world, but they're not bound to the life of this world. This is the pathway to the uncommon life: *death.* Every connection to this world that you crucify brings you one step closer to the uncommon life.

Everything to Lose, Everything to Gain

It's no easy thing to lose our lives in this way. You see, we are born into this world carrying baggage that was packed by our parents, grandparents, society, culture, and history dating all the way back to Adam. Then we pick up more as we move through life. By the time we meet

Jesus, we're so loaded down with stuff that it's a wonder He can even find us under it all. And yet He still says to us, "Come." Why? He knows that you can't handle all that baggage. He knows that you can't unload the stuff you do know about, let alone the hidden things that you don't know about. Think about it. If you could fix your own life, then Jesus could have stayed in heaven with the Father. The Cross wouldn't have been necessary, and Satan wouldn't be as bold as he is. But, praise God, He did come, because *"the things which are impossible with men are possible with God"* (Luke 18:27).

So, how do you lose your life? How do you get rid of all that baggage that hinders you from achieving that uncommon life? You start on a journey with God in which He reveals Himself in a divine process that involves **Redirection**, **Risk**, **Requirement**, and **Reward**.

Redirection. It all begins with a call—a call that usually reaches us in the midst of our commonness. Have you heard it? Perhaps you were in church, or maybe you were reading, praying, or listening to the radio when the word of the Lord came to you, beckoning you on to some phenomenal thing, giving you a vision of something beyond who you are or what you're doing. In that moment you looked at your life and said, "God, I'm willing. God, I want something great to happen. God, I believe You." Your faith was high. But then you got back to your real life and your real circumstances. The kids needed a ride to soccer practice. Your checkbook statement came and needed to be balanced. All the leaves came off the trees during the night and now you need to rake your yard. All this stuff in your life began competing with your faith.

You're saying, "God, You've called me to be great," while you lug those bulging garbage bags down the driveway. "I'm a man of purpose" doesn't sound quite so impressive coming from the guy running the leaf blower along the sidewalk. "I'm a great woman of God" sounds funny coming from a mother focused on wiping applesauce out of her toddler's hair.

You know that God has called you to greatness, and you promise Him that you'll spend time with Him in prayer about it as soon as you send out that memo, do the laundry, wash the car, pick up groceries, supervise that employee, feed the family, pay the bills, and find the remote control...again.

You might be in school saying, "God, I want to do something great, but I've got finals coming up. I've got mid-terms coming up." And the Lord help you if you're trying to have a move of God in your house when you have a new baby! The baby is not concerned with how great you are. He doesn't care about your needing time to do some serious prayer, fasting, casting out, and around-the-clock binding and loosing. That baby just wants to know when the next bottle is coming!

People who are called to live uncommon lives receive the call while they are doing ordinary things.

Your individual circumstances may not match any of those scenarios, but most of us can certainly identify some stuff in our lives that competes with and crowds out our faith. But, do you know something? Those things don't negate our call!

When I started looking through the Bible, I found that those people who were called to uncommon lives received a call while they were doing ordinary things. While they were taking care of the daily routines of living, God gave them an invitation that would redirect their lives. Take Moses, for example. He was out on the backside of a desert mountain watching sheep. What's more ordinary than that? David was doing the exact same thing when Samuel came to anoint him to be the next king of Israel. Then there's Elisha. Before he received the double portion, he was plowing in the field. What could be more mundane than that? A couple of men were fishing when Jesus called them to become disciples. In another instance, the men weren't even fishing. They were fixing nets when Jesus walked by.

All of these people—and many more—were simply doing the ordinary things that normal people do when God tapped them on the shoulder and told them they could be something great. In the middle of doing their daily work; in the middle of operating in their vocations, taking care of business—somewhere in the middle of all that—they received an invitation that said, "In the midst of what you're doing, I'm going to open up a space to you. I'm going to open a door for you. I'm going to open up your mind and your heart so that you can see that the place you're in is not an accident. I'm about to change your life so that all you've been doing becomes a jumping-off point to launch you into greatness."

That's how it starts. God will meet you on your road and redirect your focus. He will show you something that will reveal His potter's wheel in that daily grind. But, you've got to have a little bit of spiritual curiosity. You've got to be willing to investigate like Moses did. Even though Moses was taking care of the sheep that day like he always did, he wasn't so focused on daily life that he missed God when He showed up. That burning bush caught his attention. It caught his focus. Now I understand that it's not uncommon to see a bush on fire in that part of the world because of the extreme heat and dryness; but Moses was curious, Moses had his eyes open, Moses had his attention turned up all the way. He kept looking at the bush and, as he did, realized the fire was not consuming it.

The Bible says that Moses made a conscious decision to *"turn aside"* (Exod. 3:3) and see what was going on. Moses was curious and he was blessed for that; the payoff for spiritual curiosity is divine revelation. When something catches our spiritual eye, and we investigate, we receive something that confirms God's desire to redirect us. When Jesus spoke to the fishermen, they didn't ignore Him. They followed Him and became fishers of men. When the angel of the Lord came to Mary, she didn't ignore his greeting—and she received the privilege carrying the Savior in her womb.

When we stop and pay attention to God when He speaks to us in our ordinariness, He gives us vision. He causes us to see, not so much with our natural eyes, but with spiritual perception, that something uncommon, something great, can come of our lives. God knows that what we see is extremely important. If we see ourselves as defeated, we'll be defeated. If we see ourselves as never being able to achieve, we will never achieve. If we see ourselves as always being under, we will always be under.

Now, I'm not talking about self-help or positive thinking. This is not some Little-Engine-That-Could philosophy, or some doctrine of positive mental attitudes. I'm talking about more than that—I'm talking about *vision*. Vision and positive thinking are two different things. Positive thinking is you trying to picture something and you attempting to achieve what you picture. Vision is God's invitation to a fresh perspective—a perspective that shatters your present reality along with all your thoughts concerning it. In the midst of your ordinariness, it tells you, *"Eye has not seen, nor ear heard, Nor have entered into the heart of man the things which God has prepared for those who love Him"* (1 Cor. 2:9). Vision is not about you coming up with what you want to be when you grow up. It's about you discovering what God has laid up for you, which you can see only by following Him in faith.

Vision is God's invitation to a fresh perspective.

Risk. Once God makes it clear to you that He wants to redirect your life, He will always introduce an element of risk. That's where many of us jump ship, because we like to be safe. We like to be careful and prudent. We like to figure it all out ahead of time. On the other hand, I'm not suggesting that you just carelessly throw your life to the wind. There needs to be a certain amount of planning because it is unwise to start building before counting the cost. However, if we allow that way of thinking to restrict us, it will keep us from walking by faith.

Now, it's easy to risk all when we don't have anything. But the older we get, the more we accumulate, and the more comfortable we become, the harder it is to risk the good we have in order to gain something great. Nevertheless, if we want to get out of common living and enter a life of miracles and overcoming faith, we must be willing to risk.

This pattern holds true for the uncommon heroes of the Bible. For example, God told Abram to leave his father's house and go into a land that God would show him later. (See Genesis 12:1.) That's how God does it. He says, "Let go of this first, then I will give you what I promised you." Jesus told Peter to step out on the water if he wanted to get to Him. Peter left the boat, and when he did Jesus was not within reaching distance. In essence He said, "Walk away from the boat. You have to take some steps where there is nothing to hold on to but My promise."

It's easy to risk all when you don't have anything.

The children of Israel took those steps across the wilderness between Egypt and the Promised Land. David spent years fleeing and hiding in caves between his anointing and appointing to the throne. Even Jesus endured three lonely days separated from the Father between His death and His resurrection.

Risk is what separates you from your common life and thrusts you into your uncommon one. When you're willing to risk, you send a clear message to God that you trust Him. You also send a message to yourself that God is worth trusting.

Requirement. Closely related to risk is requirement. Risk speaks of what you give up. Requirement speaks of the One who receives what you're giving up. On the way to the uncommon life, God will always take you through seasons of requirement. Now, we don't talk too much about requirement in churches these days because it makes people nervous. We like to think that, as we go through every season in our life, God will give us whatever we want without obligating us to give anything to Him. If you think this way, you're deluding yourself. In order to get where you're going, every so often God will give you a season of requirement.

What exactly does that mean? In other words, this is the season where God tests your devotion to Him and your belief in your call to greatness. He may ask you to give up everything in your life at once, but usually He'll pick one thing at a time. For instance, He may start by talking to you about your relationship with your boyfriend or girlfriend. Would you give up that person to serve Him? Or would you sanctify that relationship, make it holy for Him? Then He might start asking you for possessions. Can you give up that sporty, chrome-covered car? Then there's your time, your money, and maybe even your children. He even may require your career status or your ministry authority in exchange for humility.

Seasons of risk prove your devotion to God. Seasons of requirement prove your lack of devotion to yourself.

Seasons of risk prove your devotion to God. Seasons of requirement prove your *lack* of devotion to yourself. The Scripture says that you overcome by the blood of the Lamb, by the word of your testimony, and by not loving your life to the death. Jesus said that if you're going to follow Him, then you need to pick up your cross and follow Him; but if you hang on to your life too hard, you will ultimately lose it. On the other hand, He said the one who is willing to lose his life will save it.

The best way I know how to say it is like this: Sometimes we don't experience miraculous, uncommon living because we love our lives too much. We like the way we've organized it. We've finally got it just the way we want it. We've got the right friends. Our finances are stable and our careers are on track. Even if our lives are not all together, we still love the fact that we control it. We get to make all the decisions. That's the crux of the matter. We don't have miracles because we would rather run the show and hire God only as a consultant and trouble-shooter.

It's time to ask yourself some hard questions. Who is keeping you from following Jesus? Whoever it is, you must love them more than you love Jesus. Whose approval do you need? Why do you have to have those people's permission to live the uncommon life? What is occupying most of your time and attention? What consumes your energy? Why do you have no time for God, no time for faith, no time for fellowship, no time for worship, and no time for prayer? If you're not giving at church, what are you doing with the money that belongs to God? What do you have that you can't let go of, even though you know it grieves God? Who do you need to let go of? What do you possess that God can't point to and say, "I require that"? Maybe you love your life too much.

Reward. Somewhere down the line in a season of requirement, we have to be willing to trade what's in our hands for the promise of what's in God's hand. And what's in His hand is our reward. This is not a reward in the sense that we did something to deserve something. God doesn't owe us anything. But, He has given us His word from Genesis to Revelation that we are His children and heirs. His reward is His Spirit, His name, His divine nature, His provision, His protection, His glory, His peace, His love, His riches, His heart, and His eternal life. His promise to Abram is His promise to us: *"I will make you a great nation; I will bless you and make your name great; and you shall be a blessing"* (Gen. 12:2).

You are God's marvelous creation. He made you to show forth His glory. He's called you to the uncommon life of power, miracles, and faith. I pray that you will allow God to speak to your heart about the greatness He wants to birth in you and through you. I believe God desires for the uncommon life to become commonplace among His people. He is ready and willing to prepare you to walk in all that He has prepared for you.

2
This Is Your Wake-Up Call

2
This Is Your Wake-Up Call

———◆◆◆◆———

I can see, and that is why I can be happy, in what you call the
dark, but which to me is golden. I can see a God-made world, not
a man-made world.
—Helen Keller

Therefore He says: "Awake you who sleep, arise from
the dead, and Christ will give you light."
—Ephesians 5:14

The Christian life is a life of progression. We walk in
light and understanding from glory to glory, from
faith to faith, and from strength to strength (2 Cor.
3:18; Rom. 1:17; Ps. 84:7). With that in mind, we have to
remember, when we talk about the uncommon life, dying
to self, and Christ living in and through us, that we are in
a progressive and continual state of "waking up." In other
words, we are getting our eyes opened to new truths all
the time. We are learning things that we didn't know about

before. Now, all things earthly have a place of origin. So it's not like these things never existed before; they were there all along. It was just that we were "asleep" to them until God brought us to a place of understanding, a place where our spiritual eyes were opened and truth was illuminated.

This is an important principle to know when you're trying to make sense out of concepts like destiny, purpose, miracles, faith, and wisdom. You are always "waking up" to see something new that will straighten your path, sharpen your view of it, or expose a trap or snare on it. So often we hear the word *enlightenment* from theologians and New Age disciples. Unfortunately, it has lost some of its weight and significance as a result, but enlightenment is the way of the Holy Spirit. He continually and gradually enlightens us to the truth about God.

We cannot contain the glory of God without adjusting our insides.

Everyone was fond of mimicking Jack Nicholson's character in the movie *A Few Good Men* when it came out. In the powerful climax, his character barks out, "The truth? You want the truth? *You can't handle the truth!*" We're in the same situation with God. He knows that we want to know Him; however, He is Truth. And our finite, weak, frail bodies of clay can't handle His holy infinitude. He's too big. Our very universe is swallowed up in the smallest particle of Almighty God because He is without bounds. Yet we say, "I want to know You, Lord. I want You to live in me," like it's nothing! There is no way we can contain the glory of God without any adjustment to our insides. So let me mimic the movie's most famous line: *You can't handle it!* Nevertheless, God, in His infinite mercy and compassion, has made it His business to enlighten us, gradually, in a progression, so that we can endure His visitation. This Christian life we are involved in is a fruitful journey by which we are always coming into greater light, greater knowing, and greater wisdom. Thus it is important that we understand the nature of this journey, lest we be in danger of missing the arrival of our destiny.

The Beginning

We first begin to wake up at the point of our salvation. Now, let me interject something here. Salvation is past, present, and future. We have been saved, we are being saved, and we will be saved. It is ongoing and ever unfolding. It is what Paul meant when he told us to *"work out your own sal- vation"* (Phil. 2:12). What I'm talking about here is the point at which you woke up to the truth that Christ is the Savior. You realized that He was the One standing at the door and knocking, so you opened up your heart and let Him in. You became enlightened to that truth. Your eyes were opened and you were born from above, or born again. It was an enlightening in your mind and in your spirit.

Salvation manifests itself in stages in your life.

The event of salvation produces a radical change of thought, which we call repentance. Repentance then produces regeneration. Regeneration brings us into conversion, and conversion leads us to sanctification. Then sanctification ultimately ushers us into glorification. You may already know these basics, but I'm trying to bring home a point: You are on a journey. Salvation manifests itself in stages in your life. To say that you are saved doesn't mean that you can point to any particular date on the calendar, paste a star on it, and declare that was when everything God planned to do in you was completed. It's important that you grasp this truth. So often, Sunday in and Sunday out, people go to church thinking that praying just one prayer at the altar means that everything God would ever do in their lives was done instantaneously. Not so.

That ought to bring some comfort to you if you think you're not God's child just because you have some things that you're still struggling with. On the other hand, don't get too comfortable. It is work when God walks you and works you through the process of salvation and unveils His will for your life. But it all comes down to this: You must respond when He gives you your wake-up call.

We need to wake up. Ephesians 5:14 says, *"Awake, you who sleep."* It literally says, "Let us wake up." I find that interesting. Don't you? What that verse is saying is that there are times when God enlightens us, and there are other times when we're to enlighten or wake ourselves up. We know that salvation begins with God. He's the One who enlightens us to it, but after that point, the book of Ephesians says (and it was written to Christians!) that there comes a time in our lives when we have to wake ourselves up.

Salvation begins at a definite period in time, as we've said, but it is ongoing and "flowers" over time, becoming fuller, deeper, and more mature. But that fullness, depth, and maturity do not happen without our participation. In other words, salvation is God's invitation to be in relationship with Him and to partake of His divine nature. He never imposes it on us. We have to participate in the process in order to enjoy relationship with Him and partake of His nature. We have to wake up and learn and grow.

Participate and Pursue

You may ask, "How do we participate if we're supposed to die to ourselves and give up control?" That's where the waking up comes in. It is not our job to make anything happen. The extent of our participation is *letting* things happen. You're not supposed to try to invent your destiny; God has already put your destiny in you. He has put His plan and His will in your spiritual DNA and charted out every moment of your life for you. Thus the more you understand that you are on a journey with God that is already mapped out, the more you'll learn to be at peace with what God is doing.

We have to wake up and learn and grow.

You'll quit trying to make yourself righteous. You'll quit trying to make yourself be strong. You'll quit trying to make God do something, move something, or change something. You'll stop trying to make other folks do things. You'll stop worrying altogether about other folks fighting you!

The problem we face from time to time is assuming that, because we can't see what God is doing, that He isn't doing anything. On the contrary, God is always doing something. We're just not always awake to it. We can't always see that He is working in us, for us, and through us, so we become concerned. We don't know what He's up to. But, God says, *"My thoughts are not your thoughts, nor are your ways My ways"* (Isa. 55:8). That is not some kind of admonition that says you will never understand what God is doing. Rather, it says that you won't always comprehend what He is doing at the moment you want to...but He will eventually enlighten you. You will begin to see.

Let me clarify something for a moment. When I said our participation extends only as far as "letting things happen," that doesn't mean we can run over to the couch, prop up our feet, and wait for a window of heaven to open up above our living room. Don't try and excuse yourself by saying, "Pastor Pitts said to quit doing stuff and let God do it." I'll tell you right now, if you try that, it won't be long before your wife walks out on you because the bills aren't paid.

No, letting God do what He desires to do in your life doesn't mean that you just sit there while He moves you like a marionette. Rather, you "let" Him in the sense that you join Him in what He's doing instead of asking Him to join you in what you're trying to do. When God shows you a business opportunity, you work at that instead of asking Him to help you get a raise on the job you're sick and tired of doing. You let God have His way—you yield to Him—and His way will always involve you getting involved, because it is through your participation that you begin to see Him more clearly.

Join God in what He's doing instead of asking Him to join you in what you're trying to do.

Your participation also shows others that God is at work in your life. Remember, God is a Spirit. He doesn't walk around on earth in plain view of everybody. If you aren't lifting a finger to do anything, then how will anybody know that He can have His way in your life? People who don't know God can't see Him; they see Him in you. Take stock of yourself right now. What do people see when they look at you? Do they see a God who is trying to hustle and work one plan or another and is always worried about what's coming next? Or do they see a God who has already called the end from the beginning? Do they see Jehovah Shalom, the God of peace, or do they see Jehovah Chicken-With-His-Head-Cut-Off? Which do you portray?

Let God enlighten you! Now, that also means you have to respond to the light you see. Jesus said in John 8:32, *"You shall know the truth, and the truth shall make you free."* So it's not just the truth, but the truth that you *know* that frees you. Obviously, if you don't know something, it's not going to help you. At the same time, only the light that you acknowledge and use is the light that will change you. Waking up isn't going to matter if you don't open your eyes and get out of bed, is it?

What do people see when they look at you?

A Little Bit of Light at a Time

It's time to wake up. Usually, when people want to be awakened, they will use some kind of alarm. There are all sorts of alarm clocks out on the market today. Personally, I think some people must like to be terrified out of their sleep if they use those foghorn-like alarms. I have never liked to be jolted from sleep. I'd rather have my alarm set on some sort of soothing music. Many times when I'm traveling and staying at a hotel, I won't use the alarm clock provided. I know I'd mess it up trying to set it. Instead I usually call down to the desk and ask for a wake-up call. I like it much better when the phone rings the next morning and a nice, pleasant voice says, "Good morning, Mr. Pitts. This is your wake-up call." "Thank you very much. God bless you," I reply. Everything is very civil, very nice. I know some people need those alarms that sound like the house is going to fall in, or one of those wind-up clocks that sound like someone dropped all the pots and pans on the floor at the same time. But I don't like those alarms. They startle me. Hearing something like that first thing in the morning can mess up my whole day.

My point is this: The type of alarm you need is related somewhat to the soundness of your sleep. You see, God is sending us wake-up calls all throughout our lives. Sometimes we can hear it and it's like easy listening music. "Thank You, God. I got that. Amen. I receive that. The truth is mine, hallelujah." Have you ever gotten a truth nice and easy like that? It's wonderful, isn't it? Then there are times when, because of the depth of our sleep—some of us actually bordering on comatose—our wake-up call has to rattle and vibrate everything around us before we rip ourselves free of our slumber.

Most of us live in a "comfort zone" that lies between the fear of failure and the fear of success.

Many of us don't like getting those kinds of wake-up calls because they come while we're in something we mislabel our "comfort zone." That's a lovely phrase that doesn't really mean a whole lot, because if the truth were told, a comfort zone is usually not that comfortable. Let me tell you what the comfort zone really is. Most of us—not all of us, but most of us—live between two points: the fear of failure and the fear of success. Whenever we get too close to either really failing or really succeeding, we don't know how we'll manage it, so we pull back into the middle and call it our comfort zone.

We live right there between failure and success and claim it's comfortable when all it really is, is familiar. In other words, we understand it. We can control it. We're used to it. We feel safe in it. That's not where the uncommon people in the Bible walked with God. When God walks with people, they wake up to what God has already ordained for them and they jump out of the middle to head for success! Don't let the familiarity you're so comfortable with keep you away from something better—something that you would already be familiar with if you had heeded your wake-up calls. God is not leading you to a place that He is inventing as He goes along. No, He's taking you somewhere that He has already declared is a part of your destiny. It already exists. It was in the mind of God before you were in the mind of your parents.

Don't let familiarity keep you away from something better.

We've got to get to the place where our "comfort zone" is the will of God, no matter how uncertain and "on the edge" that place may be.

When we wake up to what God has been telling us and respond to His light, we will find that it is actually more comfortable to walk in that light than to stumble around in the dark. So often we don't realize how exhausting it is to walk in the dark without Jesus, under the weight of our own clumsy plans for our lives, until we unload them and start letting God work out His plan for us.

It's amazing how we don't realize how much we needed deliverance until after we've got it. I remember walking through an airport one day, on my way to visit a particular church. Somebody was coming to pick me up, and for whatever reason I had a bunch of bags on that trip. I had one on my shoulder and one on each arm, and I was carrying these things through the airport. When I got outside, the gentleman who was picking me up approached and took my bags first thing. As soon as he relieved me of my load, my arms went limp like spaghetti. I didn't realize how heavy my bags were until I stopped carrying them. Sometimes we don't realize how heavy the stuff is that we're dealing with until we unload them, and then we exclaim, "Man! I didn't realize how that was holding me down. That thing was really stretching out my life and wearing me out."

If God doesn't expect us to complete all His plans at the same time, why do we try?

Part of the reason we have so many problems in life is that we're trying to do everything. What makes us think we can handle everything at once? If God doesn't put all of His plans on us at the same time, they why do we think we can handle even the smallest plan without Him? Only God, who is light, can see everything throughout eternity. We certainly can't. Our spiritual eyes can handle only so much light at a time. Have you ever shined a bright light into someone's eyes after he's been in the dark? It's blinding. He can't see anything. That's why you have to let your eyes adjust to small amounts of light at a time if that light is going to be effective in helping you see. Otherwise, the light doesn't help you see. It just hurts. In the same way, enlightenment is for our benefit.

God wakes us up moment by moment, day by day, from revelation to revelation. You see it in both Old and New Testament accounts. Abram was seventy-five years old when God called him. It was about another fifteen years later when he became "Abraham," the father of a multitude, and it was still another ten years before he learned that He would produce that multitude miraculously. Peter didn't understand in totality when Jesus said, *"Follow Me, and I will make you fishers of men"* (Matt. 4:19). But he received enough enlightenment to say, "I'm going to do that." He didn't really know what "doing that" meant, but he had something in him that recognized Christ when others didn't. After a time, he learned that if he would preach Christ and not run away as he had in the past, then the Jewish nation would receive salvation. That happened on the Day of Pentecost in Acts chapter 2. But it took quite a few more chapters before he learned that that same anointing would cause the Gentiles to be saved. God came to him in a dream and gave him a wake-up call. He told him that the Gentiles needed salvation, too. Where would we be if Peter hadn't responded to that call?

My point is, throughout your life you are continually awakened to new truths all the time. And each new truth, if you accept it, will propel you closer to God's will for you. Each time you reject it, or replace it with a lie, you block your own path and darken your own way.

Waking the Dead

Let's go to another familiar Scripture passage: John 11. We are all probably familiar with the story of Lazarus being raised from the dead. However, I want to examine four principles in this account that bring clarity and substance to the issue of waking up and walking in enlightenment.

> *Now a certain man was sick, Lazarus of Bethany, the town of Mary and her sister Martha....the sisters sent to Him, saying, "Lord, behold, he whom You love is sick."*
> (John 11:1, 3)

Now let's jump to verse 11.

> *These things He said, and after that He said to them, "Our friend Lazarus sleeps, but I go that I may wake him up."*

In verse 1, Lazarus is sick. In verse 11, Jesus said that Lazarus is asleep and that He's going to go and wake him up. Now let's look at verse 4:

> *When Jesus heard that, He said, "This sickness is not unto death, but for the glory of God, that the Son of God may be glorified through it."*

Remember, there are four principles here that will illustrate the significance of what God is trying to do with you by exposing you to the light of His truth.

Principle #1:

Faith chooses progress and doesn't get bogged down with the process.

The first thing you have to understand when walking with God is that you're not going to understand everything.

Settle that in your heart and mind. You see, if you get too concerned with *how* and *when* God will do something, you will get so overwhelmed with process that you'll miss progress. Faith, on the other hand, sees the end from the beginning. In other words, when faith starts, it sees the end, not the middle. When you walk in faith, when you remember that *"all things work together for good to those who love God, to those who are the called according to His purpose"* (Rom. 8:28), then when anything happens in life—good or bad—you know it's going to be okay; you know God is going to use it somehow in his awesome plan for your good and His glory.

Victory and defeat have nothing to do with circumstance. They have everything to do with attitude and spirit. You show me someone who believes the Word that he is more than a conqueror,

> *Victory and defeat have to do with circumstances.*

and I'll show you someone who will be victorious, no matter what the circumstances look like. Show me someone with his chin in his chest, and I can put an X in the loss column before that person even takes on his challenge.

I can't be so concerned with process that I miss progress. I don't always know how God will do what He said He would do. But, I do know that before it's all said and done, all things will work out for my good. I know that if I'm in it, I am going to win it. So no matter what situation in life you face, you've got to choose your faith and the God of your faith. Your faith is not denied reality. Your faith is a bridge over reality.

Jesus never denied that Lazarus was sick. Jesus said that *"this sickness"*—He acknowledged that there was sickness—*"is not unto death."* He then said that God wanted to get some glory out of it. So the sickness was not the end; it was a bridge that transported everybody involved across reality and into glory.

Principle #2:

Glory grows as glory glows.

This sickness is not unto death, but for the glory of God, that the Son of God may be glorified through it.

(John 11:4)

The word *glory* can mean "to step high above." It also can mean "weight or heaviness." But, in this passage, *glory* has to do with a high opinion that you have of something. In other words, the amount of glory that you give to God is based on your internal opinion of Him. Since your opinion of Him is favorable, you give Him glory. This passage also is speaking directly of Jesus. Jesus said that the sickness occurred so the glory of God might be revealed, and by it, or through it, He, meaning Jesus, would be glorified.

Here's the crux of this second principle. Whatever opinion you have of God may be good, but it's incomplete. Christian eyesight is ever unfolding. There are things about God that you don't know yet. If you knew some of these other things, you'd be giving Him more glory than you already do. You might be shouting louder and jumping higher than your neighbor right now, but you could jump to the moon and God still would not have all the glory due Him. That's why God will take you through certain situations; they will expand your opinion of Him. He will use a circumstance to bring to light an aspect of His personality you didn't know about so that, at the end of it, you'll have a greater opinion of who He is.

To bring something to light means to bring it to a place where you can see it. There are things about God that we don't know yet. We have to have our eyes opened to them. Sometimes we run into what we think is a weapon formed against us, and all the time it's actually something God was using to open our eyes to a new truth or characteristic about Him that we didn't know before. Afterward, we have a greater opinion of who He is, and He gets more glory from us. Simply put, the more of God's glory we see, the more we give Him, and the more we give Him, the more we are able to see.

> *The more of God's glory we see, the more we give Him, and the more we give Him, the more we are able to see.*

Take a look at it another way. We don't know everything there is to know about God, so He has to unfold it to us. That means we don't know everything there is to know about ourselves either, because we are constantly being conformed into the image of Christ, whom we don't know fully. When adversity strikes we tend to think that God wants to show us what we're made of. Instead, God has put us in a spot to prove that He is greater in us than we think. He uses a difficult circumstance to wake us up to some things we didn't know about ourselves.

Maybe your opinion of yourself is too confining for what God wants you to do. Maybe it is holding you back and restricting you. Now, you don't have a problem with it.

You're fine with who you are. But God has bigger plans for you than you do, so He will expand your opinion of yourself by expanding your perception of Him in you. He will make His glory grow more in you so that it can glow more in you.

Principle #3:

The testing of your faith always takes you further than what you already know.

When He heard that he [Lazarus] *was sick, He stayed two more days in the place where He was.* (John 11:6)

Jesus heard that His friend was sick, and He waited around where He was for a couple more days. By the time He got to Lazarus' house, the Bible says Lazarus had already been dead and buried for four days. When this passage began, it clearly stated that Lazarus was sick. It didn't say anything about death. The man was just sick. Jesus was the one who brought up death: *"This sickness is not unto death."* Every once in a while, the Lord will wake us up in situations to reveal Himself in ways that are impossible to explain beyond, "Look at God!" However, in order to say even that, we have to be able to hear Him above the noise of our own fear. Sometimes it is about more than expanding our understanding of Him or teaching us something that will cause us to give Him more glory.

Sometimes God will put you in a squeeze, so to speak, to prove whether you believe everything you've been saying about Him. Do you really believe He will supply all your needs? You'll find out when you lose the means you've been using to meet your needs. Do you really believe that He will deliver you from every arrow the enemy shoots at you? What will you do when you see the arrows coming and watch a few of them hit you? Will you believe He will deliver you from what you thought was a fatal wound?

This was the dilemma Mary and Martha faced. They had called on Jesus because their brother was sick. They both believed that if Jesus had been there, Lazarus would not have died, and they each told Jesus so. *"Lord, if You had been here, my brother would not have died"* (John 11:21, 32). They had seen Him heal people. They had seen lame folks walking and blind folks seeing. They knew about men and women who had been sick for years, yet healed in an instant by Jesus. They knew He could have saved their brother. Jesus knew they knew it. Their faith was already strong enough to believe Him for healing, but He wanted to take them to another level. In order to do that, He had to take them past their understanding.

Sometimes God will put you in a squeeze so you can prove that you believe.

Jesus waited until Lazarus died because, if He had come before that, they wouldn't have had any greater opinion of Him than they had before. A healing might have impressed some people in the neighborhood who didn't know Him, but He wanted God to be glorified in everybody's eyes, including those of Lazarus, Martha, and Mary. They needed to know that He was more than just a healer. In fact, He told Martha, *"I am the resurrection and the life"* (John 11:25). That was her wake-up call. If Jesus tells you something about Himself, you can bet that His goal is to prove it to you. If He wakes you up and tells you He's the Prince of Peace, expect a storm. If He tells you He's Lord of Lords and King of Kings, you'd better bow before you get humbled. He told Martha that He was the resurrection and the life—and Lazarus was dead and buried.

The Lord took the situation beyond their ability to think, work, pray, or shout their way out of it. Then He showed them what happens when He is allowed to have His way in a situation that seems beyond salvaging. And this brings us to our fourth and final principle.

Principle #4:

Roll away the stone.

In verse 39 of John 11, Jesus told them to take the stone away from the entrance to the grave. Up until this point, everybody is functioning according to previous revelation. Everybody is doing what he knows to do based on past experiences. Based on what they knew, they wrapped the body and laid it in the grave. Then everyone gathered at Mary and Martha's to cry and mourn. Now here came Jesus telling them to stop what they're doing and roll away the stone.

The theological implications of this scene have to do with the old covenant being rolled away, and with it the legalism and religiosity of that covenant. The practical implication, however, is this: If something is dead, it is unenlightened, uninspired, in darkness, and can't be called out into the light of God's Word because there is something between it and that Word. That's what the stone represents. There are parts of our lives that we have blocked off from God's Word, and therefore they can't come into light.

There are some areas of our lives that we have given up for dead. We've signed the death certificates, wrapped them up, buried them, and put a stone in front of them declaring the finality of our decision about them. There they sit in the dark, separated from the One who can give them life. You know that Jesus is the Savior, that He is a Healer. But until you roll away that stone, you're never going to find out that He is the Resurrection and the Life.

That marriage situation is going to stay in the ground and rot until you move the rock of your unforgiveness and let Jesus call forth restoration. It's not those who hear the Word who see change happen, but those who do the Word. Many people are connoisseurs of preachers and messages and books, but they don't do what they hear. You can hear a thousand messages on blessings that won't do you as much good as would three Sundays of giving your offerings. You've got to *do* something.

Until you roll away the stone, you aren't going to find out that He's the Resurrection and the Life.

If you will quit complaining about why you can't tithe, quit bragging about not knowing the Word, and quit exalting your carnal ways as "just being real"— if you'd just roll away the stone—there is nothing Jesus can't call forth.

God has the ability to mold us and make us and to produce in us a greater capacity for enlightenment. That's why those who are born again are referred to as those who walk as in the day. That's why the Bible tells us, *"Arise, shine; for your light has come"* (Isa. 60:1). *"The entrance of Your words gives light"* (Ps. 119:130). It's the entrance of it, not the hearing of it.

"Your word is a lamp to my feet and a light to my path" (Ps. 119:105). One day you'll stop trying to figure everything out and make a decision for progress, no matter what the process is. You'll learn to trust Him when you can't track Him. I've learned how to say yes when I don't even know what the question is. When Jesus said, "If you follow Me, I'll make you...," I said yes, but I didn't know that He was going to take me through all that He has in order to make me. He's still working on me, but I have learned to thank Him for the good times as well as the struggles, because He continues to make all things work out for my good.

David learned how to bless the Lord at all times. We would do well to lift up our hands and shout, like David, because we believe that God is going to jump into the midst of whatever we're in. We would do well to praise Him because, before it's all said and done, we're going to know something about Him that we didn't know before. Our faith is going to produce some confidence, and that confidence is going to work some endurance. And endurance is all we need, because the gift of eternal life is given to the one who endures.

Wake up and endure.

3
The Heart of the Matter

3
The Heart of the Matter

----◆◆◆◆----

When I think of God, my heart is so filled with joy that the notes fly off as from a spindle.
—Joseph Haydn

Create in me a clean heart, O God, and renew a steadfast spirit within me.
—Psalm 51:10

Most of us know the story of Solomon, who succeeded his father David as king of Israel. We know that the Lord came to Solomon in a dream one night and asked what He could do for him. Now, many of us can't be trusted with a heavenly blank check. We'd be asking for cars, boats, Swiss bank accounts, perfect children, trash that takes itself out, and a few other things that haven't even been invented yet. But, the Bible says in 2 Chronicles that Solomon asked God for only one thing—wisdom to rule God's people. God was so pleased at that request that He gave him that as well as everything he didn't ask for.

Scripture says Solomon became the wisest man who ever lived. What made him wise? The answer is found in the 1 Kings account of this incident.

> *At Gibeon the* LORD *appeared to Solomon in a dream by night; and God said, "Ask! What shall I give you?" And Solomon said..."Give to Your servant an understanding heart to judge Your people, that I may discern between good and evil. For who is able to judge this great people of Yours?"* (1 Kings 3:5–6, 9)

Here it says Solomon asked for an *"understanding heart."* That word *understanding* literally means "listening" or "giving undivided attention." Solomon asked God for a heart that would give Him his undivided attention, one that would listen for and listen to instruction and direction. What kind of heart you have is critical. Romans 10:10 says, *"With the heart one believes unto righteousness."* If you want to live the uncommon life, then you must get your heart right first. Miracles come to those whose hearts are right. You can't successfully kill self, or the carnal nature, unless your heart is right. Your new spirit man can't shine through until the heart is right. That's why, when God wants to get your life in order, He'll deal with you at the heart level.

The kind of heart you have is critical. It's what's in our hearts that defines who we are.

We talked about enlightenment in the last chapter. That enlightenment comes to effect a change in us, and God shines His light into our hearts first. Why? Change comes only when the heart is affected. Proverbs 23:7 tells us why: *"As* [a man] *thinks in his heart, so is he."* It doesn't matter what we say or do. It's what's in our hearts that defines who we are.

Going Below the Surface

God deals with every man, every woman, every boy, and every girl in the entire world, and it's very interesting to watch how He gets everyone's attention. He does it by speaking to who they are, not who they present themselves to be. After all, how much respect would you have for a God who couldn't see past the front you put up for people? I've seen people who appear to have everything together in front of other people, but when God starts talking to them, that façade quickly crumbles. I've seen strong men break down and cry when God deals with their hearts. I've witnessed Him deal with teenagers so strongly until they have such a strong sense of pur- *Do you need* pose that they keep away from the foolish- *a touch from* ness of the day and withstand every tempta- *God? You've* tion and tempter surrounding them. *got it.*

God is no respecter of persons (Acts 10:34). If He sees somebody with a heart that needs fixing, He's not concerned if that person is rich or poor, polka dot or plaid. Do you need a touch from God? You've got it.

It is remarkable that, as different as we are, when God starts putting His hand on us, we all start saying the same thing. We all start speaking the same language. "It's time for me to get right." "It's time for me to get my things in order." "I've got to start considering my ways." But that, my friend, is only the broad beginning. That's simply the beginning of the work that needs to be done. In fact, that's the easy part.

You look at your life and say, "I've really got to get this thing together." When you say that, usually you're referring to things you can see like circumstances, finances, and romances. You decide that you're going to serve the Lord and not the devil. You're going to give a little more at church. But, as time goes on, God gets deeper and deeper into you, and things start to get a little uncomfortable. It stops being about how you spend your money or treat your wife, and becomes more about you. Naturally, those things matter, but you always can blame somebody else for those things. You can fake your way through marriage, as tragic as that is. You can even try to buy yourself some holiness through your giving on Sunday. But the longer God puts His hand on your heart, the less squirming room you have. Sooner or later, He's going to start pointing to things that don't have anything to do with anything else except you and your evil heart.

The longer God puts His hand on your heart, the less squirming room you have.

Even when your exterior is looking calm, cool, and collected, God will have you in fits inside with questions like, "Why did you say you would get back to Sister so-and-so, then throw her number in the trash?" "Why are you praying with that brother and lusting after him in your heart at the same time?" "Why did you make such a public spectacle of that big offering you gave?" "When was the last time you visited your mother in that fancy rest home you put her in?" "Why won't you open your mouth and praise Me like you usually do? Is it because Mr. Tall, Tan, and Terrific is standing next to you?" "Are you fasting to crucify your flesh, or to show it off when you drop fifteen pounds?"

David said that God knew what he was thinking even before the thought entered his head (Ps. 139:2). He prayed that the words of his mouth and the meditation of his heart would please God (Ps. 19:14). You see, David found out that he could keep up the appearance of a solid, secure, serene life. He knew that the average person could look at him and assume that everything was fine. But he knew that on the inside, in his heart, God was seeing what was really happening. David knew personally that it was possible to smile in somebody's face and murder him in your heart. He had learned that God is not impressed by grinning faces that cover up garbage hearts. So he prayed that God would clean him up at the heart level.

You can keep up the appearance of a solid, secure, serene life, but God knows what's on the inside.

God is waiting for you to pray that same prayer. *"Let the words of my mouth and the meditation of my heart be acceptable in Your sight, O LORD, my strength and my Redeemer"* (Ps. 19:14). Yes, God loved you enough to save you. Yes, He wants to spend eternity with you in heaven. But because He is so good, and because He wants the best things for you, the Father will go through the trouble of making your way straight on your way to heaven. He will knock down every wall and every stone that separates you from knowing Him and loving Him completely. He will loose every chain that binds you to anything other than His will.

It's no accident that the Bible speaks so much about the heart. It was an unbelieving heart that kept a generation of the children of Israel from entering the Promised Land. We are told that we should guard our heart with all diligence, for out of it proceed the issues of our lives (Prov. 4:23). We are told that we will be whatever is in our hearts—we will live it out in one way or another (Prov. 23:7).

I like the way David said, in Psalm 57:7 (KJV), *"My heart is fixed, O God, my heart is fixed."* He wasn't saying that if a heart is broken, God would fix it—although that is true. Here *fixed* means to be permanent. It means to be unmoved. It means to be singular in your devotion, to come to a place where your heart is completely in God's hand and you're okay with that. When your heart is fixed, God can maneuver and massage your heart and challenge you on issues that nobody else can challenge you on, and you're surrendered and submitted to that. You want Him to deal with your attitudes and your intentions. You desire the light of His Word to expose the dark places in your heart that are hidden from the world, and sometimes even from you.

To live the life God has called you to, your heart must be fixed on Him.

In order for us to live the life God has called us to, one where the extraordinary is ordinary and the supernatural is natural, our hearts must be fixed on Him. Have you ever seen one of those nature shows where the cheetah is about to attack a gazelle? The first thing you notice is that the cheetah's eyes never leave the gazelle he has chosen for his dinner. Before he takes off running, he's looking at her. As he picks up speed, he's got his eyes fixed on her. When she starts to run and dart to the left and the right, his eyes follow her every movement. That's how our hearts are to be fixed on God. Running or standing still, our hearts are focused on Him.

Because God is infinite and impossible for us to know completely, we can be captured by Him even as we chase after Him. It's like being in love. The person you love has you. You're not going anywhere. But every day you want to find out something more. You're chasing after that person with your heart even after you have given him or her your heart. That's why folks can be married for forty years and say they're more in love today than they were when they first got married. Are you more in love with Jesus today than when you first said yes to Him?

Are you more in love with Jesus today than when you first said yes to Him?

Fixing a Fixed Heart

When you come to the place where your delight is in the law of the Lord, when you come to the place where you are submitted to God's hand on your heart, then something begins to work. By the way, no matter how uncomfortable it gets, it is much better to know that God is working on you. You should be really scared when He leaves you alone to work on yourself.

Let's go back to our story about Solomon. The young king asked God for a listening heart. That was his invitation for God to speak to his heart. Speaking to our hearts is how God gets them in order. He speaks to them, through them, about them, and into them. He speaks *to* the heart in the context of relationship. He speaks *through* it in our relationships with others. He speaks *about* our hearts in His Word, and He speaks *into* our hearts when He puts that Word in us to reinforce truth, or to rebuke lies.

When God takes on the task of fixing our hearts on Him, His goal is to make us more capable of receiving Him into them. Remember, *"as* [a man] *thinks in his heart, so is he"* (Prov. 23:7). The more God you have on the inside, the more like God you become on the outside. I'm not talking about just good behavior. I'm talking about godly behavior. By fixing your heart on Him, God can make your heart sensitive to Him. He will sensitize it to His voice, His leading, His warning, and His warmth.

The more God you have on the inside, the more like God you become on the outside.

The Bible often speaks of a hardened heart as well. That is a heart that God is either not dealing with or has left off dealing with. It is one that has become so used to its own ways that it has begun to make excuses for the way it lives, and those excuses drown out the voice of God. Saints of God are not immune to this phenomenon. In fact, we are particularly prone to it, but God has a way of plowing up hard ground and bringing us into a position to hear what we would not hear before.

When you were first born again, you had a pure heart. All you wanted to do was be right in the eyes of God. You just wanted everything to be okay. You were just glad God saved you from your mess. You were quick to apologize to people and quick to repent. Isn't it amazing that, after a while, the excitement of being a new believer wears off and all that repenting starts to make you feel "unsaved"? It's at this point that folks start wanting to repent in private. Apologies are replaced with excuses and self-justification. All of a sudden it's somebody else's fault that you had to cuss him out. And that person has to come up with an excuse about how you made him do that thing that you cussed him out for. Then, if you get into a spirit of anger, you'll start finding Scripture verses to support your evil behavior. That's when pride creeps in and you're too busy *being* God to hear God. Your heart becomes hardened.

God is still talking to you, but you don't hear Him because of the hardness of your heart. He is saying you should humble yourself and ask that person to forgive you, but you have already claimed your right to your anger and you can't hear Him. Perhaps your pastor didn't speak to you last Sunday, so you talked about him to everybody who would listen from Monday to Saturday. Now it's Sunday again and God is telling you to confess that sin, but you don't hear Him.

Once your heart gets hard, you get stubborn. And once you become stubborn, you become stiff-necked. Then you become rebellious, and that is as the sin of witchcraft and idolatry in the eyes of God (1 Sam. 15:23). Why is it like witchcraft? When you are in rebellion, being stubborn and hard-hearted, not hearing the voice of God, and you still come into the house of the Lord, throw your hands up in the air, and act like God is in charge of your life, you're lying. You know that the only god you're serving is yourself. Rather than serve God and repent, you'll try to conjure up a blessing by dancing and shouting false praises from the same mouth that cursed the pastor and his family all last week.

You've got to let God get a hold on your heart and stop trying to act like you can walk upright when your heart is crooked and bent. I know you think you've got it all together, and maybe some of the people around you think everything is pretty wonderful in your life, too. But let's get serious. Take a minute right now and sincerely ask God to do whatever He must to create a clean heart in you. Ask Him to expose anything in you that is not like Him and to wash it away. Now, before you go on, let me warn you. If you sincerely pray David's prayer for a clean heart, God will surely grant you that petition, and He won't go back on it even if you change your mind down the line. I promise you that He will fix everything that needs fixing—including some things you don't even know about.

Stop trying to act like you can walk upright when your heart is crooked and bent.

Perhaps, on the other hand, you're saying, "My heart doesn't need to be fixed; it's just fine." That's great. But while you might find that you don't have any big issues of the heart to deal with, God is always willing to fine-tune you if you will let Him. And one of the first places He'll start is at the level of your motives.

How you respond in certain situations is often a good indicator of the contents of your heart. You might say, "Well,

I had anger in my heart toward another person, but when I saw him, I just smiled and acted like nothing was wrong. How is that an indicator of the contents of my heart?" My answer would be that you lied. Your response was to lie, to cover up sin, and that response came from your heart. The other person might never know you as anything else but a nice person, but God would call you a liar. My point is, when God gets to fine-tuning you, He starts taking the covers off of all your wicked motives, not just your wicked behaviors.

I do have some good news, though. Although God deals with us personally, and sometimes independently as it relates to certain matters, He never deals with us unfairly or subjectively. He doesn't treat us any differently than He does someone else. He has certain universal guidelines that, when He is dealing with us, when we are learning how to guard our hearts and protect our relationship with God, we can use to see whether we're on track. We find those guidelines in His Word.

Keep Your Balance with the Word

The Scripture can get deep, but it also can be used the way a child uses training wheels on a bicycle. In other words, before a child learns how to ride properly and without any help, training wheels help him find his balance without falling and getting hurt all the time. In the same way, God gives us His Word so that while we're learning to listen to the voice of His Spirit in our lives, we have some parameters to help us maintain our balance. If we get used to what He says in His Word, then we can handle, without falling, things that He has not specifically talked about.

Let me explain. There are certain things regarding general principles of godly living that are in the Bible. But every issue you'll encounter in your life isn't found there in specific form. If you have three job offers, the Bible doesn't have chapter and verse on which offer you should take. If you have two godly, Spirit-filled people who want to marry you, the Bible doesn't tell you which one to pick. Neither does the Bible tell you how many children you're supposed to have.

Learn to know the voice of God. Listen to Him, and everything will work out for you.

You need to learn to know the voice of God before you get to those intricate and specific issues. Meanwhile, you must learn how to balance in the things of God with those training wheels. Let Him put some guidelines in you so that you know what it feels like in your heart when you're trying to make something be God that isn't, or trying to rebuke something that is God. Learn to know the difference.

Have you ever tried to make something be God's will when you knew it wasn't His will? You got your friends to agree with you, and you talked yourself into it. You even mustered up a goose bump when you talked about it. You really worked that thing—you kept saying it was God, and saying it was God, and saying it was God, and all the time you knew it wasn't God.

Then a little something popped up in your heart that you knew wasn't there a moment ago. God sent you a spiritual email that said, *"Trust in the LORD with all your heart, and lean not on your own understanding; in all your ways acknowl-edge Him, and He shall direct your paths"* (Prov. 3:5–6). Here's a principle of the kingdom. Listen to God, and everything will work out for you. So often people don't want to hear that. Why? Because if you listen to God, He might tell you that you can't have that thing you want. So you tell your-self, "No, that can't be God. That isn't God. I bind that! I cast that thought out of my mind. I stomp it under my feet, get it behind me, or whatever else I have to do. But that word has got to go. I do not receive that!" You may not receive it, but that doesn't mean it's not addressed to you. And that doesn't automatically erase the return address on it. It's still from God.

He puts things in us so that when He allows things to be put before us, we have the capac-ity to respond correctly and keep our-selves in check. His Word is there as a safety device, because there is nothing in it that violates anything that God will tell you. Yes, God does deal with us personally, but He always deals with us according to and consistent with Scripture. He is not going to say anything that contra-dicts what He has already said.

> *God always deals with us according to Scripture. He will never contradict what He has already said.*

I've heard all manner of things over the years that people have tried to tell me the Holy Spirit told them, even though God told everybody something else in His Word. Here are a few examples.

People have come up to me and said—even though they were married and had children and a job—"The Lord told me that I'm supposed to leave my family and go preach to the nations." No, God didn't say that. God said that you are to "leave and cleave." His Word tells us to leave our father and mother and cleave unto our spouse. He told husbands that they should dwell with their families. He told wives that they were responsible to their husbands and children first. If God called you to preach, then He's God enough to work out the logistics of it without violating His Word. He knew you were married when He called you. And He didn't call you to break up your family to go fix somebody else's.

Some people got fired because they had a forty-five-minute lunch break and they didn't come back for three hours. Why? They claimed, "The Holy Spirit told me to intercede." That wasn't the Holy Spirit. If the Holy Spirit wants you to intercede for three hours, He will pick three hours that belong to you and not your boss. Don't go around testifying that the devil attacked you on your job for praying, when the truth is he just set you up for failure, and you helped him do it. He was trying to pull you back into poverty, and you gave him the rope.

Here's one of the biggest deceptions I hear. People fall in lust with each other and walk around saying, "The Holy Spirit told us it was okay for us to have sex because we love each other. We're not married yet, but we are going to be. We're married in the eyes of God, who calls the end from the beginning and those things that are not as though they were." No, in the eyes of God, you're in fornication. In the eyes of God, you are in sin. In the eyes of God, you need to go to the altar and tell that person to loose you and let you go. Stop all that touching and agreeing; the Holy Spirit is not in that!

Sometimes people tell me that God told them that they are not supposed to tithe for a season. "We're supposed to hold on to our tithe for a season so we can—quick, fast, and in a hurry—get out of debt. We're really doing it so that later on we can give more." Be careful! You open yourself up to the influence of some wicked spirits when you start attaching God's name to your own agenda. When you start trying to twist Scripture around to get what you want, you are causing your heart to become vulnerable to unclean spirits. After a while, you won't be able to tell the difference between the voice of God, your own voice, and the voice of the enemy.

Sooner or later, you've got to let God be true and every man a liar. Even if God's Word cuts your flesh, even if it requires you to do something it pains you to do, don't lie against God. Don't open up your mouth deceitfully and say that God has blessed you to do something evil.

> *Let God be true and every man a liar.*

When you start attaching God's name to things that He didn't say, then you place yourself—or the enemy, or that lover, or that preacher, or that friend—in the place of God. That takes you right back into the witchcraft of rebellion again. It's no less rebellion just because it looks nice to everyone else. Your motives are as visible to God as your methods. To His eyes, what you believe is as obvious as how you behave. Your purposes are as clear as your practices. Remember, He sees your heart, when other people only see your habits.

God's greatest desire is to have your whole heart. What does He want to do with it? He wants to repair it, restore it, refresh it, and make you into a man or woman who can receive every blessing He has stored up for you. There are some blessings God can't give you because your heart is too small to receive them. How do you give a loving husband to a woman who hates herself too much to trust his love? How do you give millions to a man with a poverty mentality? How do you bless a church with a new building when the heart of it, its membership, is too afraid to worship freely? How do you give a flock of sheep to a pastor whose covetous heart is too focused on the preacher down the street with the fancy new car?

If we are to become a people who desire the will of God and live the uncommon life, we must be willing to let God do whatever it takes to make our hearts ready to receive His will in its fullness. We've got to let Him get our hearts right.

4
Matters of the Heart

4
Matters of the Heart

◆◆◆

Compassion is not a snob gone slumming. Anybody can salve his conscience by an occasional foray into knitting for the spastic home. Did you ever take a real trip down inside the broken heart of a friend? To feel the sob of the soul—the raw, red crucible of emotional agony? To have this become almost as much yours as that of your soul-crushed neighbor? Then, to sit down with him—and silently weep? This is the beginning of compassion.
—Jess Moody

Anxiety in the heart of man causes depression, but a good word makes it glad.
—Proverbs 12:25

*H*ave you ever looked at people and just knew, before they even said a word, that something was wrong? Or you knew, just by the expression on their faces, that they had gotten some good news, heard a good joke, or needed a good shoulder to cry on? If you're a parent, do you often know when something is going on with your kids before they even have a chance to say hi when they come home from school? And have you ever had a boyfriend or girlfriend say, "We need to talk," and you knew a breakup was imminent before the talking even got started?

It all comes back to the heart. We could probably take an untold number of books to discuss the heart and still not cover all its aspects—let alone try and cover everything in one chapter! But because this issue is so important, and because I believe we need to understand the part it plays in both motivating and hindering us on our journey as we navigate this Christian life, I want to focus on the heart some more in this chapter.

We have to learn to deal with each other.

We've already learned that God speaks to our hearts and that it is at this level that change is born. We don't become more godly because God spoke into our ears or presented something that our eyes observed. We don't change because we touched something or because our minds simply remembered an event. No, it's the heart. Paul said it is with *the heart one believes unto righteousness*" (Rom. 10:10). We realized that it can be difficult to hear God if our hearts are hardened by stubbornness, bitterness, or pride. And we know that God will never tell our hearts anything that conflicts with His Word. All of what we discussed in the previous chapter explains how God deals with our hearts and the behaviors that flow out of them. But, we're not God in that we can see in people's hearts, and we have to learn how to deal with each other.

First Samuel chapter 16 finds the Lord instructing Samuel to go to the house of Jesse to anoint one of his sons to be the new king of Israel. David was out in the field taking care of the sheep when Samuel asked to see Jesse's sons, so the prophet viewed all the other sons first. When he saw Eliab, the prophet thought he had surely found the Lord's anointed.

> *But the* Lord *said to Samuel, "Do not look at his appearance or at the height of his stature, because I have refused him. For the* Lord *does not see as man sees; for man looks at the outward appearance, but the* Lord *looks at the heart."* (1 Sam. 16:7)

There are two principles in this verse. The main principle is that God looks at the heart. The second is that man looks at the outward appearance. Now, please don't overly spiritualize that second point. It is perfectly legitimate for people to form impressions of you based on what they see. When you go for a job interview, that potential employer is probably not going to ask you about your good heart. He's looking at your résumé, your behavior, your poise and confidence, and possibly your clothes.

Man looks at the outward appearance. God looks at the heart.

Some people form impressions about you because of a haircut or the condition of your shoes. I've known of women who refused to go out with a man because he was wearing the wrong kind of watch, or who agreed to go out with another because he drove a nice car. Some men get so caught up with how a woman looks that they don't care what she thinks or how she feels, or even *if* she thinks or feels anything. Why is that? God says it's because man looks at the outward appearance. If that's true, then what's the big deal? If God says we're focused on the outward man, then who are we to argue with Him? But look closer at this passage. God told Samuel that man's tendency is to look at the outer appearance, but He wanted Samuel to operate contrary to man. He told him not to look at Jesse's sons with his fleshly eyes.

When we become born again, one of the first things God wants to do is give us a new perspective. He wants us to get used to seeing things the way He sees them. He wants us to get used to seeing people the way He sees them.

We can see what's really going on inside a person's heart if we look with God's eyes. He wants us to be conscious of the fact that man looks at the outward appearance and not to be surprised when people form their opinions of us based on what we appear to be. At the same time, He expects more from those of us who call ourselves His sons and daughters. As His children we have His Spirit in us, and that Spirit guides us into all truth. That means we can know what's really going on inside a person's heart, even if his lips are telling us something different. We can see that heart with God's eyes.

It's interesting to note how this all happens. A carnal man, one who relies on his fleshly nature, forms his impressions of a person based on what he sees, then from there makes assumptions and draws conclusions about what must be going on in that person's heart. He starts from the outside and works his way in. A man or woman who moves by the Spirit of God does just the opposite. A man of God looks on the inside and works his way out. You see, the Spirit of God in you will break through all the façades people have put up to block you from seeing who they really are and will deal with every issue from a place of truth and not facts. At that point the outward appearance simply becomes punctuation for whatever statement the heart makes, as opposed to defining its content.

People have hurt my feelings more than once. As a pastor, that's unavoidable. Some people think they can say anything to pastors and it will just roll off our backs and leave no scars. That's not true. But, more often than not, I find that when people hurt me like that, it's usually because there is something hurting inside them. The appearance of their anger is punctuation for some hurt that their hearts are trying to express. I had to learn to look for the pain in the other person and not be so focused on my own that I neglected to see where he needed my intercession.

> *With the Spirit of God, a person's outward appearance simply becomes punctuation for whatever statement his heart makes.*

Think about it. If you're dealing with people from the outside in, instead of the inside out, then all your prayers for them will be selfish and self-serving. For example, if you hurt my feelings and I decide to pray about it, then my prayers have to go past just asking God to keep you from being mean to me. Even if He does answer that prayer, what have I accomplished besides making myself free from pain? You might go out tomorrow and hurt somebody else the way you hurt me. On the other hand, when you pray for those who hurt you, you have to address their need, not your own. You have to ask God to show you what's in their hearts that made them treat you like that, then pray for their healing in that area. You have to love them enough to want their hearts to be fixed. And you have to love the people they affect enough—even if you don't know them—to protect them from the same pain you have suffered. In order to do all that, you have to see as God sees.

God wants us to love Him, but He also commands us to love our neighbor as ourselves. Wouldn't we rather be understood without always having to explain ourselves? Don't we want to be accepted without having to become something other than who we are? Wouldn't we rather that people see our pain and be sensitive to it without our having to scream "ouch!" because they accidentally poked a place that wasn't quite healed? Don't we want to be loved unconditionally and uncompromisingly? Don't we want people to see our hearts and not always our habits? God says that all of that is not only possible, but also that it is His desire for us. He wants us to love one another the way He loves us. And He loves us from the inside out, not the outside in.

God loves us from the inside out, not the outside in.

I believe that the Holy Spirit wants to show us how to see into and handle the hearts of the men and women we encounter on our way to the uncommon life. I believe part of the perfecting work of the Holy Spirit involves teaching us that the condition of a man's heart does more to define who he is than anything else. Then we don't just analyze actions; we discern intents, needs, and desires. Proverbs

15:13 says, *"A merry heart makes a cheerful countenance, but by sorrow of the heart the spirit is broken."* In other words, the condition of a person's heart will show up in his or her appearance, if we will see it.

At your next opportunity, look someone in the eyes, and you will begin to see true indications of what is in his heart.

A Merry Heart

Now, let's turn to Proverbs 17:22:

A merry heart does good, like medicine, but a broken spirit dries the bones.

I believe in being happy. Don't you? I also believe that we ought to have a good time and rejoice in the Lord. Even modern science and medicine tell us that a happy, peaceful life is more healthful! They know that many diseases and disorders are related to the inward emotional state of a person. Stress, for example, aggravates almost any condition, while peace and pleasure *A happy, peaceful life is more healthful.* help reduce the destructive effects of many illnesses. Isn't it wonderful that psychologists, physicians, sociologists, and relationship experts are finally catching up to what God has already said in His Word?

The human heart really has a vast capacity to express a wide range of emotions. It also is mysterious in its operation. I think we all are sometimes astounded at the depth and power of people's passions and feelings, both good and bad. I am sometimes amazed at how benevolent and altruistic some people can be. And I have been equally amazed at the stubbornness, bitterness, and cruelty of people.

The Bible tells us that a merry heart does for us what good medicine does. As I studied that passage, I started thinking about the ability of our hearts to be joyful, elated, or filled with gladness. Now, first of all, I don't think that joy is related to owning material possessions. Unfortunately, there is a pervading notion in America that if people can acquire enough, know enough, or do enough, that their hearts will be more joyful. That's simply not true. I have spent a lot of time in Nigeria preaching, and the people there don't have most of the things we say we can't live without—things like transportation, education, medicine, and health care. Yet, the people of God, I noticed, would walk for miles to church and sit all day long, and their hearts were still filled with joy. They sang, danced, and gave praise to God for all that He had given them, even though they didn't have a lot of what we would call the necessities or the niceties of life.

A joyful heart does not come from material possessions.

I also have spent time preaching and teaching the people of Bulgaria during a time of intense struggle and political unrest. The entire population didn't have heat because the government shut it off the across the nation on selected days to conserve energy. The people of Bulgaria just had to hope that the weather was warm that day. But when I was there, it was not warm, and they didn't expect it to warm up for another month.

These people didn't have any heat in their houses. They would get up in the mornings, have a little cold egg, a little piece of cheese, and a little hard piece of bread, and call it breakfast. They would wear their coats in the house and wrap themselves in blankets, even when they went to bed at night. Despite all that, though, the people of God would leave their houses and brave the cold to go to church. The praise and worship leaders, wearing coats and winter boots, would lift up mitten- and glove-clad hands unto the Lord and sing, "Hallelujah, for the Lord our God, the Almighty, He reigns!" Their merry hearts cut through the cold and you could see it on their faces.

Another time I was in Durban, South Africa, which is really the epicenter of the AIDS epidemic. It's estimated that fifty percent of the people in Durban are infected with that deadly virus. Everywhere you go, you are surrounded by death. Every day you see someone's funeral procession or someone's burial. So many people are dropping over, weak or close to death, that they can't find enough places to put them. And yet, when you enter the churches there, you find brothers and sisters with praise in their hearts and unfailing faith in the midst of so much death. They say, "God will turn it around."

I said all that to illustrate that a merry heart doesn't have anything to do with what you've got in your garage. It doesn't have anything to do with your zip code or your bank account. A merry heart is not the exclusive property of those with a closet full of clothes or a refrigerator full of food. Rather, a merry heart will clothe you with peace and patience when you have to wear the same dress every day. It will fill your belly with contentment until bread reaches your hand. It will lift your spirit and cause you to walk with a little pep to catch the bus or even while you walk to work. It will put a smile on your face in the unemployment line. A merry heart will shrink a tumor that radiation has been powerless to stop, and it will have you praising God from your own sickbed. A merry heart is good for whatever ails you.

Sometimes we can be guilty of complaining when we don't have anything to complain about. Sometimes we can be guilty of feeling sorry for ourselves when we don't really have much to feel sorry about. The truth is, if we think about it, God has been good to us. We don't have to think about it for very long either. God has been so generous, kind, and merciful. If we can't see that, then our hearts are not open to the truth.

God has been good to us. If we can't see that, then our hearts are not open to the truth.

One of the great characteristics of a merry heart is that it is an open heart. When your heart is open, that means you're open to people. You can receive them and give to them. You can be warm and inclusive. A merry heart is not a judgmental heart. It is not angry, harsh, evil, bitter, or envious because it is open and eager to embrace other people.

When your heart is merry, you can be generous of spirit. You will look for ways to accept people and let them know that they're okay with you just the way they are. You'll let them know that you understand that, even though they don't have everything quite together yet, there is still room for them in your heart. On the other hand, people whose hearts are closed, are very small. Their world is narrow and petty, and they hang on to everything for fear of losing something. They're afraid to let people in, afraid to be kind. They think that kindness will make them appear weak and invite people to take advantage of them. They build up walls to keep people out without realizing that they are actually building a prison for themselves.

It is also true that even a merry heart can be broken. It is not immune to pain and disappointment. When Proverbs 17 speaks of a *"broken spirit,"* it is the same as speaking of a broken heart. No matter how much we try to understand and investigate and unravel the mysteries of the heart, the cold reality is that every once in a while, the human heart gets pushed beyond its limits. The Bible calls that a broken heart.

Heart Breakers

Has your heart been broken? If your broken heart has never recovered, you need to know that when Jesus announced that the Spirit of the Lord was upon Him in Luke 4:16–19, one of the things He said was that the Spirit had anointed Him to *"heal the brokenhearted."*

Faith wanes when your heart is broken.

When your heart is broken, it becomes stretched to the point where it seems like you don't know what to do. You have nothing left to give, and sometimes don't even want to try. Sometimes you're just tired out. You've been hurt one too many times; you've suffered one too many indignities, one too many rejections, abuses, or obstructions. Faith wanes when your heart is broken. And when you have trouble believing God, you're really not interested in trusting the people around you.

I've got good news for you: Jesus heals broken hearts! The first thing He will do, however, is show you how your heart got broken in the first place. He will reveal the source of the wound so it can heal from the inside out. Let's take a look at some causes of a broken heart.

Captivity. Captivity can break your heart. Captivity is that situation or state of mind that has you feeling trapped. You're in a tight place that you can't think, move, talk, or pay your way out of. Captivity has you pressed in on every side. You're in a tight place. Have you ever felt like your life was a dead-end, your job doesn't hold any joy for you, or the people surrounding you don't refresh and nourish your spirit? They just drain you and deplete your strength. Have you ever felt like every day was just a continuation of the previous bad day and that tomorrow only promised more of the same? That is captivity, and that can break your heart.

Psalm 126 describes how the people of Zion were in captivity until the Lord stepped in.

> *When the* LORD *brought back the captivity of Zion, we were like those who dream. Then our mouth was filled with laughter, and our tongue with singing. Then they said among the nations, "The* LORD *has done great things for them." The* LORD *has done great things for us, and we are glad.* (vv. 1–3)

Look closely at this passage. It says that God's people were in captivity, but that God brought it back. That means

He rescued them and brought them out. Now look at the behavior of the people who allowed God to bring them out. They're laughing and singing, and the people who don't even worship God— *"the nations"*— know that God is responsible for all their happiness. You see, when God brings you out of captivity and heals your broken heart, people who don't even know God will testify on His behalf. That's evangelism! You don't have to hit people on the head with your Bible, rain down rebukes on them, or threaten them with the wrath of God. Just let God bring you through something nobody thought you'd get out of, and they'll praise Him for you.

There's something else you need to see at the end of this passage. It says, *"The LORD has done great things for us, and we are glad."* As I said earlier, if we would tell the truth, God has been good to us. All we need to do is acknowledge it. When Zion acknowledged the goodness of God, it made them glad. That word *glad* is the same word used in Proverbs 17:22 and translated *"merry."* So when we think about the goodness of God, it makes our hearts merry, and no matter what we're going through, a merry heart will be like medicine to us.

> *When God brings you out of captivity and heals your broken heart, people who don't even know God will testify on His behalf.*

That psalm goes on to say, *"Those who sow in tears shall reap in joy"* (v. 5). Really think about that statement. Captivity leads to a broken heart, and a broken heart leads to tears. But, the harvest of tears is rejoicing and a merry heart. In other words, every tear you cry is planted in the soil of your heart and will eventually bring forth joy. That word *joy* actually means "singing." Remember, at the beginning of the passage Zion's mouth was filled with laughter and the tongue with singing. *Joy* and *singing*—it's the same Hebrew word. Now look at the last verse in the psalm.

> *He who continually goes forth weepeth, bearing seed for sowing, shall doubtless come again with rejoicing, bringing his sheaves with him.* (Ps. 126:6)

Your tears are *"seed for sowing."* When God talks about planting and reaping, He's making promises. He's telling you something that you can take to the bank. So what is He promising here? He's saying that your tears are not wasted. He's saying that every tear you allow to fall from your eyes will bring forth its own harvest of joy. How does that happen? Go back to Psalm 126. What happened between the captivity of Zion and the singing? The Lord stepped in, and they acknowledged His work in their lives.

Your tears are not wasted. Each one will bring forth a harvest of joy.

God has a word for you: Your crying is simply His announcement that some joy is about to come your way. You see, it is His job to turn your captivity. Your job is to praise Him and talk about His goodness. If you will do your job, I promise that He will do His. David said, *"I will bless the LORD at all times"* (Ps. 34:1). Just do that, and then watch how quickly your captivity is turned around and your broken heart made merry.

Keep in mind that you have an enemy, and that enemy wants you to think that your captivity is God's word to you.

He wants you mad at God so you won't praise Him. No, that captivity is your proof that God is restoring your soul and making room in your heart to receive what He's about to pour into it! We've got to stop accusing God of being a sadistic ruler who gets some kind of perverse joy out of seeing us trapped and helpless. That is not the God we serve.

So what's the whole point? If you have ever loved anyone, then you know that relationships are forged in a crucible of crisis. You have to go through something with somebody to know that you can trust that person. In the same way, you've got to go through some things with God or you'll never trust Him. How are you going to trust His strength if you're never weak? How are you going to trust His love if you're not unlovable sometimes? How will you trust that He's merciful if you don't mess up, or His grace if you're never undeserving? You'll never trust His wisdom until you reach the end of yours, or His omniscience unless you find yourself in the dark. In other words, captivity is a necessary part of learning how to trust a God whose name is Savior.

Captivity is a necessary part of learning how to trust a God whose name is Savior.

Betrayal. Besides captivity, betrayal can cause your heart to be broken as well. Have you ever been betrayed? Have you ever had somebody hurt you and you never saw it coming because you really trusted him or her? It hit you right out of the blue and knocked the wind right out of your sails. David had to deal with that. In fact, he wrote Psalm 55 to commemorate it.

For it is not an enemy who reproaches me; Then I could bear it. Nor is it one who hates me who has exalted himself against me; then I could hide from him. But it was you, a man my equal, my companion and my acquaintance. We took sweet counsel together, and walked to the house of God in the throng. (Ps. 55:12–14)

David said he could have handled it if it had come from somebody whom he didn't get along with, but this was a friend. This was somebody whom he considered to be a companion. He may have even worked with this person. He certainly went to church with him. But this was personal. Betrayal is always personal.

Betrayal has a way of cutting you to the deepest part of your heart because you have invested a part of yourself into that relationship. You allowed that person into your heart, put your arm around him, and walked with him. He knows the intimate details and secrets of your life. You think he'll stand with you against your enemies. But when that person turns out to be the enemy—the one you didn't see coming—it puts a scar in your heart. Sure, you eventually shake it off. You get over it and you walk on a little further, but that scar is there, and you're hesitant to trust the next person who wants to get close.

If it happens time after time, deep disappointment can set in. There are so many young people growing up in our society today who deal with broken promise after broken promise, hurt after hurt. Everyone they know violates or abuses their trust. What happens to them? They grow into adults who can't be trusted, and who don't care whose heart they break. Children who are betrayed become adults who betray.

David, however, showed us how to handle betrayal. He left it up to God to take care of it.

Cast your burden on the LORD, and He shall sustain you; He shall never permit the righteous to be moved. But You, O God, shall bring them down to the pit of destruction; bloodthirsty and deceitful men shall not live out half their days; but I will trust in You. (Ps. 55:22–23)

Yes, David's warfare prayers sound as if he was being rough on those who hurt him, seeking their destruction and death; but notice that he always left it up to God to fight for him. If you think back through David's life, you'll remember that David had a few chances to kill Saul, but he didn't take them. Saul was trying to kill him, and no one would have blamed David if he had taken Saul's life. No doubt David felt hurt and betrayed by this man, his father-in-law, in whose house David had lived as a young man. Saul had been like family to David, yet David knew that any vengeance against Saul would have to be carried out by the Lord Himself. In our human nature we want to hurt the people who hurt us, but God says it's His job to punish the people who do us wrong.

Loss. A third thing that can break our hearts is loss. When you suffer a loss so great that you don't know how to deal with it—when it seems like you put all your eggs in one basket, and the devil came along and ate all the eggs and threw away the basket—the pain of it can break your heart. Maybe you have lost someone close to you, or you had a relationship—a marriage, a friendship, a child—that was taken away. You can lose a business, your status, your youth. Loss can encompass so many things.

It is the desire of the enemy to keep you in a position where you always feel loss. He wants you to believe that every time something is taken away from you, you are somehow the lesser because of it. But, it is the desire of the Holy Spirit to bring you to a place where you feel that you are always being added to, not subtracted from. You may ask, "How can this happen in the midst of loss? How do I keep from feeling like I'm at a deficit when I find myself deficient in so many areas of my life?"

The enemy desires to keep you in a position where you always feel loss.

You may know people—in fact, you may be one yourself—who can pinpoint a specific date in their lives where things began to change for the worse after a major loss. Perhaps a loved one passed away. Perhaps they lost their job. Maybe they didn't get accepted to the school they dreamed all their lives of going to, and they have lost all hope.

I met a young man one day who had put all his hopes into sports. He was a great athlete, and he was looking forward to a long career in professional sports. But, in his freshman year of college, he injured his knee in the first game. Suddenly everything he thought he had was no longer there. As a result, he became a bitter young man. He was angry, and he began to drink himself into oblivion.

This young man had his whole future planned out, and when those plans were taken away, he couldn't handle the loss. From the moment he suffered that loss, he ceased to know joy, hope, or happiness...until the moment he was born again. The Holy Spirit showed him that there was purpose in his loss, and that made him feel as though he had been added to and not subtracted from. Today his testimony is a gift to the body of Christ.

When Joseph forgave his brothers for selling him into slavery, he pointed out to them that God had allowed every terrible thing to happen to him so that by it many people would be saved. (See Genesis 45.) Joseph saw the value in losing his family, his position, and his reputation because God used the situation to help others. Because Joseph was willing to be used of God like that, he was rewarded with more than he lost. In fact, that was Joseph's destiny. His name means "the Lord will add."

Sometimes terrible things result in many people being saved.

The story of Naomi in the book of Ruth is a great study of the beautiful harvest that can come from loss. Let's take a brief look at it. The book of Ruth begins by telling us that Naomi's husband has died. Now, the name *Naomi* means "something beautiful." It literally means something worth seeing. However, in the opening verses of the book of Ruth, Naomi suffered loss. Then in verse 5 we find out that her two sons died. So here was a woman who was supposed to be something worth looking at, but has experienced great pain/loss. Remember, a merry heart gives you a joyful countenance, but a broken spirit dries up your bones.

Naomi spent ten years away from the people of God and her hometown. When she returned, the people looked at her and said, *"Is this Naomi?"* (Ruth 1:19). The Bible says everybody was talking about it. Before, when they saw her, she was something to look at. She was something to see. She had a glow about her; there was life in her. But all that loss, and all that time on top of all that loss, had changed her. The people who used to know her hardly recognized her now. Then she told them what had been going on.

> But she said to them, "Do not call me Naomi; call me Mara, for the Almighty has dealt very bitterly with me. I went out full, and the LORD has brought me home again empty. Why do you call me Naomi, since the LORD has testified against me, and the Almighty has afflicted me?"
> (Ruth 1:20–21)

You may remember the story of how the children of Israel left Egypt and came to a pool of bitter water, which they could not drink of until the Lord purified it. That body of water was called "Marah." The name means "bitterness," and that is the same name Naomi is using here. She was telling people, "Don't even call me something worth seeing, and don't call me beautiful or joyful. Call me bitter."

She had accepted a place in life in which she became bitter. She had suffered loss and had resigned herself to being angry with God and allowed bitterness to take root in her. Have you ever met someone who was so mad he didn't care if you knew he was mad? Have you ever seen somebody who has been so angry for so long that she has that look of permanent resentment on her face, which told you, "Just go ahead and say whatever you want about me. I'm bitter and I have a right to be, and I'm not changing for you or anybody else"?

It is possible to get to a place in your life where you have suffered so much that the external devastation of that situation begins to move inside you and devastate your heart. You start to look different. You don't smile anymore. The days when you were happy and carefree are just a distant memory. You barely remember the days when you had friends around you. You don't know when they stopped wanting to be around you, and you don't even know that you've driven them away with your anger and your negative personality. Instead, you think there is something wrong with all of them, and you've decided to accept the fact that you're just not going to have any friends, that you're going to be frustrated, lonely, sour, and resentful. If this is you, are you ready to hear a word from the Lord?

Just like God sweetened the bitter waters of Marah, so He can heal you or your loved one of bitterness. That's the story of Naomi. How did God sweeten her life? The events happened like this. Ruth, Naomi's daughter-in-law and the widow of one of her sons, fell in love with a man named Boaz. At the same time, Boaz fell in love with Ruth. When *Just like God sweetened the bitter waters of Marah, so He can heal you of bitterness.* Ruth told Naomi about Boaz, Naomi perked up and started giving her advice about how to act, what to put on, and so on. All of a sudden, Naomi came back to life, because now she had something to do. She had someone to help. Eventually, everything she advised Ruth worked, and she and Boaz got married and had a baby. Here's what the end of the book of Ruth says about this child and Naomi:

> And may he be to you a restorer of life and a nourisher of your old age; for your daughter-in-law, who loves you, who is better to you than seven sons, has borne him.
>
> (Ruth 4:15)

The baby's name was Obed, and the prophecy was that he would be the restorer of Naomi's life. In other words, this baby would add to Naomi's life. Here's the point. Naomi, who was something to look at and was joyful, became bitter because she thought her life was over. What she didn't know was that God has a way of restoring life, and many times that restoration comes when people make a decision to open up their hearts and give out of their hearts into somebody else's life.

Too often when we suffer loss we buy into the lie that says, "I'm in pain, so everything and everybody who comes near me has to get sucked into my pain. Then, somehow, I'll get better. I'll get over it if I can keep talking about it, keep rehearsing the heartache of it, and get enough sympathy for it." So we talk to whoever will hear us about how entitled we are to feel bad and how much right we have to our anger at whomever we think is at fault. The truth is, the longer you focus on your problem, the more that problem becomes the center of your life. The key and the answer is to get another focus.

The longer you focus on a problem, the more it becomes the center of your life. The key and the answer is to get another focus.

You see, you won't ever get your heart mended while everything has to come toward you. In other words, you are not the center of the universe. Everything does not revolve around you. You're not God, and the minute you become the center of your world, you have put yourself in His place. However, as soon as you let go of your pain and your hurt in order to sow into somebody else's life, all of a sudden something in your life is going to turn.

Take Job, for example. He suffered more loss than just about anybody whom any of us knows. Yet, the Bible says that God turned things around for Job when he prayed for his friends (Job 42:10). I understand the hurts and pains that we all suffer, and I know that they are sometimes difficult to get over. But, Jesus came to heal the brokenhearted. And the way He puts your heart back together again is by opening it up and telling you to release things from your heart again. Find somebody to bless. Find somebody else to pray for. Find something that gets your mind and your attention off of yourself. Let God take care of your stuff while you take care of someone else's. Take time to praise Him every so often. Begin to look through your life and count your blessings.

If you will do these things, then I promise that a miraculous thing will happen. Those tears you cried will begin to bring forth a harvest of joy and singing. You will find your merry heart again, and everybody who had counted you out will begin to praise God with you.

A broken heart is a necessary part of our sojourn to the uncommon life. But it is not our destination.

A broken heart is a necessary part of our sojourn to the uncommon life. If we're going to die to ourselves, God has to take us through some fire that will burn everything off of us that is not like Him. A broken heart, though, is not our destination. It is just a stop along the way. It's a place to strengthen our trust and shore up our faith. It's a place where the comfort of God restores our souls and where we learn to be content in whatever state we are in.

Finally, and most importantly, a broken heart equips us to minister to others who are suffering. The Word of God says that Jesus went through some painful things so He could intercede for us from a place of understanding. (See Hebrews 4:14–16.) If I come through, then I'm better able to help you through.

Man looks at the outward appearance, but God looks at the heart. Let God look into your heart and show you that you have amazing resilience and fortitude. He has brought you through some valleys and restored some areas that you thought were dead. Now He wants you to take your newly wrought courage and brave the depths of someone else's broken heart. He wants you to shine the light of your experience into some dark hearts and help Him break up the ground in some stony hearts.

Do you see how it works? The same "binoculars" that God uses to see into someone's heart are found in the hearts of His very own people, tried and tested by the Almighty Himself. No one is left out. He uses every fixable heart, and He fixes every useable one.

5
Show Me Your I.D.

5
Show Me Your I.D.

Be who you is, cause if you ain't who you is,
then you is who you ain't.
—*Harry Hein*

What is man that You are mindful of him, and the son
of man that You visit him?
—Psalm 8:4

How often have you asked yourself, "Who am I?" Perhaps I should ask you a different question: How many times has your answer to "Who am I?" changed over your lifetime? Before you can have confidence—before you can be a victorious, committed man or woman of God living the uncommon life—you have to settle the question of identity. Do you know who you are?

> O LORD our Lord, how excellent is Your name in all
> the earth, who have set Your glory above the heavens!

Out of the mouth of babes and nursing infants You have ordained strength, because of Your enemies, that You may silence the enemy and the avenger. (Ps. 8:1–2)

This is a sort of side note to our topic here, but do you know that when you praise God, sometimes the devil will stop whatever he is doing to you? Self-defense classes teach people that a mugger is less likely to attack a person who refuses to act like a typical victim. Sometimes the best thing to do is scream and make a lot of noise, because that can scare the attacker off. The devil is no different. He knows that noisy saints are the worst ones to pick on because they'll call down a whole host of help from heaven with their praise.

When I consider Your heavens, the work of Your fingers, the moon and the stars, which You have ordained, what is man that You are mindful of him, and the son of man that You visit him? For You have made him a little lower than the angels, and You have crowned him with glory and honor. You have made him to have dominion over the works of Your hands; You have put all things under his feet, all sheep and oxen—even the beasts of the field, the birds of the air, and the fish of the sea that pass through the paths of the seas. O LORD, our Lord, how excellent is Your name in all the earth! (Ps. 8:3–9)

God ordained the works of His fingers. Nothing is an accident. Everything that is, God has ordained. And He has given man dominion over it. Yet, the psalmist still praises God for it. God gave earth to man, and yet here we find man giving Him praise for it. When was the last time you praised God for fashioning your job, your house, or your children? Everything we own or take care of was designed and then created by God before it became ours. Everything that belongs to us belonged to Him first. That's why the psalmist began and ended Psalm 8 magnifying the name of God. And by magnifying the *"name"* of God, he is referring to all of the covenant names of God, and all that God is.

Here's the key: This is also a family name. Let me say it the way we would today: "O LORD our Lord, how excellent is Your *last* name in all the earth." It's a family name because in Him, the Bible says, the whole family in heaven and earth is named (Eph. 3:15). This is an issue of identity, because your identity has to do with your name.

Your identity has to do with your name.

Recognize Your Identity

You name something based on what it is. Titles with names represent functions. For instance, my name is Michael, but my children don't call me Michael. They call me Dad. That's my function in their lives. In the same way we call God "Lord." That title speaks to His function in our lives. When we declare that His name is great, though, we're referring to His person, not His function. When we talk about the name of God, we're talking about His identity, and by extension our own, since we are members of the family that carries His name.

When you were born into your earthly family, you became, for better or worse, identified with them. You were so-and-so's daughter, or what's-his-name's son. The identity

I want to talk about here, however, is our identity as a part of God's family. When we are born again, we take on His nature and name. But because we haven't figured out who we are in God through Jesus Christ, many of us don't live powerful, Spirit-led lives. We don't know our spiritual identity and are still searching. We have a whole world full of people trying to "find themselves." I want to tell you that you were "found" when you came to Christ!

Now, this is going to adjust your theology if you've been trained up in religiosity and not relationship. Religious people don't understand the Bible. They think that Jesus came only to show us who God is. That's part of it, but there's more. Before Jesus even came to earth, God had shown Himself to a lot of people. So Jesus didn't come just to show you who God was; Jesus came to show you who *you* were. He came to show you who you were so you wouldn't take somebody else's word on the subject. If you don't know who you are, you'll take the devil's word on it—and he's a liar.

Jesus came to show you who God is, but He also came to show you who you were.

God has made you to have dominion in the earth, but when you don't know who you are, whatever you come up with to define yourself is usually wrong. Think about it. If you go to yourself to find yourself, and you're lost, how are you going to have the answers? You're lost because you don't have the answers in the first place! If you go talk to a psychologist who doesn't know who you are in Christ, all he can tell you is dysfunctional psycho-babble and worldly labels. If you're lost and he's lost, where do you think you're going to end up? You'll wind up in a ditch. The only answer is to take your broken self back to your Creator and let Him tell you what He made you to be.

The Bible refers to Jesus as the *"last Adam"* (1 Cor. 15:45–47). The first Adam was created in a particular way to fulfill the purpose of God in his life. When the first Adam messed up, man no longer had a perfect model or example to look at in order to figure out who or what he was. Throughout history, man kept looking to imperfection to try to get some sense of his spiritual composition. Needless to say, following a pattern established by a defective template can only lead to the wrong answers. When you start at the wrong point, you're going to end up with the wrong answer. So Jesus came to show us what the perfect man is supposed to be like, so that we'd quit looking to people for our identity and start identifying with Christ.

> *If you don't know what you're supposed to be, you can't help but end up as something you're not supposed to be.*

This issue of identity may not seem important to you. After all, there are plenty of successful, happy, stable, intelligent people who couldn't care less about Christ, God, or their place in the body of believers. That is regrettable, for the truth is that they could be so much more in themselves and for others if they knew God's will for them to become a part of His family. But because they don't know who they are, they obviously have to be something that they are not. If you don't know what you're supposed to be, you can't help but end up as something that you're not supposed to be. Society will take every opportunity to tell you that if you were raised this way and that way, then you'll grow up and act this way and that way. And you won't know any differently! In other words, if they say you're supposed to be messed up, and you don't know that you're not supposed to be messed up, you can't help but be messed up!

Do you know why people have nervous breakdowns? It's because they think they're supposed to. That's what the world teaches you. If the pressure of life gets to be too much for you, you're supposed to have a nervous breakdown. If you don't get enough ice cream when you're three and somebody steals your bike when you're eight, you're supposed to be violent. If people don't treat you right, you're supposed to act up. That's what we are told. Those messages are communicated over and over again, and if you don't know who you are, you can't help but be what you're not supposed to be. Many of us are living below our Christian privileges because nobody ever told us what we were supposed to be or enlightened us about what we're capable of doing.

There's a story about a guy who lived out in the desert raising prairie chickens. He had a bunch of those little prairie chickens, and all they did was hang out there in the desert, walking their prairie chicken walk and talking their prairie chicken talk. They were just a bunch of prairie chickens going nowhere.

Then one day this man goes out and sees a baby eagle. He takes that eaglet and decides to raise it with the prairie chickens. So he takes that little baby eagle and puts him down there with the other birds. Day after day, week after week, the eaglet just followed all those prairie chickens around. He learned how to walk the prairie chicken walk and how to talk the prairie chicken talk. Then one day as that little eaglet was walking around in the field with everybody else doing the prairie chicken walk, talk, and squawk when he looked up into the sky and saw an eagle soaring with his wings spread out, doing the things that eagles do. That eaglet looked up and said, "Wow!" But then one of his prairie chicken buddies elbowed him and said, "Take your eyes off him. You're just a prairie chicken."

Many of us have been created to be eagles, but we've been walking around with so many prairie chickens that we don't know what to do. So God brings us to a place where we have to begin to recognize our identity. If that eaglet ever got it into his spirit that his destiny was not to scratch the ground, but to soar, it would change his life. Imagine how silly and out of place he must have looked walking around in a chicken yard with a seven-foot wingspan. Before you laugh at that picture, though, make sure you're soaring and not squawking and walking in places God has not called you to.

If you don't realize who you are in God, the devil can keep you oppressed.

You are connected to something far beyond what your mind can comprehend. But as long as you are not aware of that fact, the devil can keep you oppressed. If he can keep you from knowing who you are, he can keep you in captivity. It is always the responsibility of the oppressor to keep the oppressed in ignorance. Once the oppressed receive the truth, they begin to rise up and walk in the liberty that always accompanies the Spirit of the Lord.

You need to start figuring out who you are. You are vulnerable to the tactics of the enemy if you've never settled the question of your identity. Perhaps you have been raised in a church that made you feel like you were always supposed to lose. Or maybe you were raised in a society that told you you weren't supposed to expect much out of life. The enemy kept coming at you, and you kept falling for his lies because they agreed with the lies you've believed all your life. Remember, if he can keep you ignorant, you will never soar. Don't stay in that chicken run. Jesus came not only to show you who God is, but also to show you who you are!

When Jesus was tempted in the wilderness, the devil said, *"If You are the Son of God"* (Matt. 4:3, 6). Did you notice that this happened right after God had said, *"This is My beloved Son"*? When Jesus was baptized, the voice came out of heaven and spoke, *"This is My beloved Son"* (Matt. 3:17). The Holy Spirit descending on Jesus like a dove confirmed the declaration. I advise you to recognize this pattern and remember it. Whenever God tells you who you are, whenever you begin to get a revelation of who you are, the enemy and the pressures of life will always come and attempt to reduce that revelation to a figment of your imagination. *"If you are a child of God, why don't you do this?"* If we're not sure about who we are, we'll be tempted to try to validate ourselves based on our performance rather than on the proclamation of God.

One of Satan's favorite tricks is to tell us that we're something when we're not, and then make us unsatisfied with who we think we are. When we fall into that trap, we spend all our time trying to self-help our way to understanding. America sells more self-help books than any other nation in the world because Americans are constantly trying to change themselves into something they think other people will like and accept. "If I could lose a few pounds..." "If I drove a different car..." "Maybe I should have that plastic surgery." "If I could live in a different house, marry a different spouse, get a better job..." If we had the ability or capability to make our lives perfect, then Jesus could have stayed in heaven with the Father—the Cross wouldn't have been necessary. But it was necessary because we don't know who we are, let alone what we're sup-posed to become or how to attain that. And too many of us don't know that we were accepted by God before we were even born. (When you have a minute, study chapter 1 of Paul's letter to the Ephesians.) Knowing that God accepts us keeps us from chasing approval and acceptance from other people.

> *If we had the ability or capacity to make our lives perfect, then Jesus wouldn't have had to go to the Cross.*

Defined by Purpose

The Bible says that *"in Him we...move and have our being"* (Acts 17:28). It is not our doing; it is our being. God did not make us human doings. God made us human beings. Paul did not say, "I do what I do by the grace of God." He said, *"By the grace of God I am what I am"* (1 Cor. 15:10). Thus, if it's in Him that we live and move and have our being, then we will never figure out what we are, or what our being is until we understand that it's wrapped up in our under-standing of Him. In other words, who we are is founded on and defined by who He is.

Jesus did not say to Peter, "Who do you think you are?" He didn't say to Peter, "What would you like to be?" either. Jesus said to Peter, "Who am I?" (See Matthew 16:15.) Peter said—read closely—*"You are the Christ, the Son of the living God"* (v. 16). At that point Jesus turned around and said, *"You are Peter, and on this rock I will build My church"* (v. 18). You can never figure out who you are until you figure out who He is. Once you figure out who He is, then He will tell you who you are. He will tell you what your destiny is. He will tell you what you're capable of. *"You are Peter, and on this rock I will build My church...I will give you the keys of the kingdom of heaven, and whatever you bind on earth will be bound in heaven, and whatever you loose on earth will be loosed in heaven"* (vv. 18–19). Do you see how it works?

You can never figure out who you are until you figure out who He is.

Peter did not know what his destiny was. What do we do when we're don't know our destiny? We try to construct our own. We make our own plans. We write out our vision. We decide what we want to be. We want this and that in our lives. Then we take it all to God and say, "I'd like You to endorse this for me. I've got my vision; I've got my plan. This is who I'd like to be. Are You all right with me on this thing, Lord?" We waste a lot of time doing this because we don't understand that if God created us, then He made us with a purpose in mind. God had everything figured out before we even showed up, so whatever we're taking to God is destined to fail or, at best, to fall short of His plans.

If you're trying to get God to buy into your own definition of your life, then you're asking Him to trade

His identity for yours. You're asking Him to settle for second, third, fourth, or fifth best because anything you're considering for yourself is based on your opinion of yourself, or on somebody else's opinion of you. It's based on the prairie chickens you've been living with all your life. It's based on the wrong teaching you've been getting in religion, or the wrong input you've been getting from television. And so you take from all these wrong sources, use their information to formulate your plans for your life, then go to God and say, "This is what I want to be. Make it happen."

The problem is that God had already settled your purpose when He settled your identity. And His identity in you has been pushing you toward that purpose. That's what the Scripture means when it says,

> *God had already settled your purpose when He settled your identity.*

> *Before I formed you in the womb I knew you; before you were born I sanctified you; I ordained you a prophet to the nations.* (Jer. 1:5)

What God said to Jeremiah here is true of all of us. Before we were born, He knew who we would be. In fact, He formed us specifically for our purpose. He does not allow us to come into the world and then just say, "Man, what am I going to do with that one? Let's see if I can find a slot to stick that one in." God knew you before He created you. And He created you for a purpose.

One of my greatest concerns is that we have a generation of young people who have not been taught this truth.

As a result they consider their lives to be cheap because they believe that they have no future. They believe they have no destiny. They believe they can never succeed. They believe the world will get so bad that they will never be able to live into proper adulthood. They've been taught that they'll never have a happy marriage. They've been taught that their kids will probably end up wild. They've been taught that they probably won't have a good standard of living. They've been taught all of these bad things, and they have begun to believe them and act them out. Since there is no vision, their life philosophy becomes one of mere survival: "The future is dim, so why not get everything I can get now and die young?"

This curse has come upon our land because of our lack of understanding concerning our identity. The devil has sought to rob us of our identity. Some churches want to hide it under false piety and religiosity. And schools are attempting to perpetuate the lie that we identify more closely with dead apes than a living God.

The curse of evolution is certainly part of the cause for what we see happening in the streets today. You can teach people that they came from animals for only so long before they start to act like that is true. The notion of evolution disconnects man from his God-given identity and raises more questions than it answers.

"Will the thing formed say to him who formed it, 'Why have you made me like this?' Does not the potter have power over the clay?" (Rom. 9:20–21). If our "potter" was a big bang that came from nothing, then we've got problems. Our own scientists, philosophers, and evolutionists tell us that form

always follows function, that things do not develop or come into existence without a preexisting purpose or initiating force. Who "banged" the bang that put us here? And if nothing existed before it, what preexisting purpose made it necessary to bang at all? Without going into a deep discussion, there is more "scientific" evidence supporting God than there is supporting evolution.

You can be the descendant of animals if you want to, but I'm staying in the family of the Most High. My life has not "evolved." My life "revolves" around the One who created all life and who created me for His good pleasure. I don't share ancestry with creatures who can't become heirs to the throne of grace. I don't walk upright and have thumbs because my uncle was a monkey. I walk upright because Adam walked that way. Unfortunately, I'm also a sinner because Adam walked that way. And in my sin, I have tried to tell God who I am and commanded Him to get with my program.

My life has not "evolved." It "revolves" around the One who created me.

Then one day I found out that God was God, and I was His creation. I found out that everything I could dream or think or do was as filthy rags compared to what He could do for me, in me, with me, and through me. I found out that I could walk upright in more than just my flesh. I could walk upright in my spirit because Jesus walked that way. I don't know any apes that can call Jesus Lord. Monkeys are not my family. I don't take communion with chimps, and I don't know of any record of one asking "What must I do to be saved?"

I share ancestry with Abraham, Isaac, and Jacob. I will see my brother Paul and my sister Mary one day in eternity. King David and I will behold the beauty of the Lord together. I don't expect Curious George to be standing next to me shouting hallelujah. He may be curious, but he was not designed to seek the Lord.

You're not a monkey. Nor are you a "junkie," a "problem child," a "slow learner," an "at-risk youth," or a "manic depressive." If that's what you're calling yourself, then you're lying to yourself. How do I know that? Because it's hard to be all that stuff. You see, everything that God makes, He makes for a purpose. And everything that He makes can fulfill that purpose *easily*. That is so contrary to what we normally think. We've been trained in religion to think that everything has to be hard. That way we can feel better when we accomplish it, like we did something. But Jesus said, *"My yoke is easy"* (Matt. 11:30).

When God created a bird, He did so for a purpose—so it could fly. For that reason, everything about that bird is geared toward flight. A bird's bones are lighter, and they're even hollow in some places. Feathers, body outline—the whole anatomy of the bird is geared toward flight. It is not hard for a bird to fly. It's hard for a bird to *walk*, but not to fly.

Fish don't have to hold their breath. They just move in that water. When you jump in to that water, you're just splashing around. Even if you know how to swim pretty well, you're still not a fish. You may think you're doing all right, but compared to a fish, you're like a big clumsy turtle. As a matter of fact, even a turtle can out swim you.

A guppy can out swim you. It was made for swimming, so it swims—easily.

It's not hard for a cow to give milk. It's not hard for a pig to get fat. It's not hard for a skunk to stink. None of this stuff is hard. And here we are—the only living creatures on the planet laboring. "What are you doing?" "I'm trying to be somebody." We need to quit trying, sweating, toiling, and striving. Because if we ever figured out who we were, and that we were created for a purpose, like the fish that takes to water and the bird to the air, we would just start walking into the plan of God for our lives. We would start doing it effortlessly. Once we know who we are, we won't receive another lie about ourselves.

Once we know who we are, we won't receive another lie about ourselves.

Go Back to the Source

If you really want to know what something is, you need to go back to what it's made from. Genesis chapter 1 tells us, *"In the beginning God created the heavens and the earth. The earth was without form, and void; and darkness was on the face of the deep. And the Spirit of God was hovering over the face of the waters. Then God said, 'Let there be light'"* (Gen. 1:1-3). Guess what happened when God said that? There was light. There was no big wrestling match. There was no battle between darkness and light to gain control of the earth. When God said, *"Let there be light,"* there was light. God then said the light was good.

After that God said He wanted *"a firmament in the midst of the waters, and let it divide the waters from the waters"* (v. 6).

In other words, He wanted waters above and below the clouds. *"Thus God made the firmament, and divided the waters which were under the firmament from the waters which were above the firmament"* (v. 7). When God said, *"Let there be a firmament,"* it just happened (see verse 6). Clouds don't have to work to stay up there. The sky is not falling.

Next God said, *"Let the waters under the heaven be gathered together into one place"* (v. 9). You know, it's not hard for the ocean to have current. It's not hard for the ocean to be wet. It's not trying to be wet. It didn't wake up in the morning and say, "I need to make sure I stay wet today. Let me make some waves so people will know I'm an ocean." It's not trying to do anything. It just is.

Next God says the earth should bring forth grass. You see, now that God has the elements together, when He wants something He just speaks to the elements that it's made from and commands those elements to bring it forth. God doesn't say, "Let there be plants"; He said to the earth, *"Let the earth bring forth..."* (Gen. 1:11). The Bible reports that the earth did what He asked.

God spoke to the earth. Why? It's because the earth is capable of producing all of these things. Because in their basic element, all these things are made from the same thing the earth is made from. God simply speaks to what He wants something made from, that it bring it forth. Keep going in Genesis, and you read that God wanted some stars. What did He do? He didn't say, "Let there be stars." Rather, God talked to the firmament...and the firmament brought forth stars. The firmament is made up of gases, and that is what stars are made of. God also spoke to the water to bring forth fish. So you see that the elements were already there. He just spoke to the source.

Then we come to the part where God wanted you and I. And when God wanted us, He did not speak to the ground. Neither did He speak to the firmament. Instead, *God spoke to Himself.* God said to the ground, "Bring forth fruit." God said to the water, "Bring forth fish." God said to the firmament, "Bring forth stars." Then He said, "I'm getting ready to do something really big. What do I want this thing made out of?"

He didn't speak to the ground. He didn't speak to the firmament. He didn't speak to the water. *"Then God said, 'Let Us make man in Our image, according to Our likeness'"* (Gen. 1:26).

If you don't know who you are, then it's because you haven't figured out your source yet. Do you believe the lie that you came from a monkey? Then you'll act like one. Do you believe that you came from dirt? You will act like it. It's about time somebody told you where you came from so you know who you are. *"O LORD, our Lord, how excellent is Your name."* We all have the same family name, which means we came from the same source.

Perhaps you are saying right now, "Okay. But man was made from the ground." Yes, but man wasn't *created* from the ground. People haven't been taught properly about this. There is a part of you that's created and a part of you that's made. We're talking about the part that was created. God *made* man out of the dust of the ground. Then God put what He *created* inside what He made. You're so busy looking at what God put you in that you haven't tried to figure out who you are. But you can't look at a package and know what's inside it. A box of cereal may have a picture of what's inside, but if I'm hungry, I don't eat the box. I've got to go inside to get what it is.

We have all kinds of people trying to define who they are based on their package—black, white, Hispanic, old, young, rich, or poor. You don't really know who you are. That's why you keep throwing out those different labels when people try to get to know you and find out who you are. That's why you keep stocking yourself on the shelves of life next to other packages that look like your package. You're just going by labels and packaging and don't realize that inside that package is what God created.

God doesn't have anything we need. God is everything we need.

When God formed you out of the dust of the ground, He breathed into that package the breath of life. God put what He created inside of what He made and determined that man was created in His image. He purposed that man would have dominion because man's source was God.

Are you trying to get something from God that you already have? Are you saved and filled with the Holy Spirit, yet still trying to get something from God? Here's something else we need to consider. The problem is that God doesn't *have* anything. God *is* it.

God doesn't have love; He *is* love. God doesn't have power; He *is* power. God doesn't have light; He *is* light. Consider the podium that sits at the front of most churches. Many of those podiums are made out of wood. Now, a tree is not made out of wood. A tree *is* wood. So if a podium is made from a tree, then it can't help but be wood. It isn't trying to be or get wood; it *is* wood because of its source.

Take holiness, for example. So often we go to God and say, "Oh God, You're holy." That's true. He is holy. He doesn't have holiness; He is holy. We, on the other hand, are all trying to *get* holy. That doesn't work. We don't *get* holy. We don't *acquire* holy. We have to *be* holy.

God didn't say to you, "Do holy." He didn't say, "Go get some holiness in you." He didn't say, "Find holy." No, He said, "Be holy." When He said, "Light be," light was. When He said, "Earth, bring forth," it brought forth." So how can He say to you, "Be holy"? It's because He knows who you are. He knows that you came from Him. And since He is holy, then you are holy too, because you came from a holy source. In fact, He says, "You be holy, even as I am holy." (See 1 Peter 1:16.) God says, "You've got to be it, because I am it. And I'm the source from which you came. Everything that I am, you already have. You don't have to come get it. You don't have to go find it. You have what I am." Glory to God, I have what He is!

Now, the devil will try to tell you that you're low down, broke, defeated, and discouraged. As a result, you'll try to go get happiness. You'll try to get joy. But in God is the fullness of joy (Ps. 16:11). You already have joy, because He *is* joy.

The devil also came and turned you upside down and made you think that you *have* a spirit, when you don't have a spirit. You *are* a spirit. I don't have a spirit; I am a spirit. Don't get so wrapped up in dealing with the package that you start to think you have something when you are it. You are a spirit because your source is spirit! *"God is spirit"* (John 4:24). A podium made from a tree has got to be wooden; a man made from God's essence has got to be spirit. A man's got to be spirit because his source is Spirit!

When you get a spirit man from a spirit God, the devil will try to turn him upside down, so that he won't know who he is. In that case, rather than living as a spirit that possesses a body, that man will live like a body who possesses a spirit. But thank God for Jesus. He turns everything right side up, and that spirit man gets up and says, "Now, I am what God made me to be."

I'm done with believing lies. It's too exhausting trying to be something that I'm not. Aren't you tired of it too? Maybe somebody told you that you were an alcoholic. Maybe somebody told you that you're just like your uncle or your daddy, or that you're like this or that. They simply didn't know what to call you because they didn't know where you came from. You didn't come from alcohol. You didn't even come from your daddy. Before He formed you in your mother's womb, God knew you. You had life with Him before you had life on earth. Life began for you when God began. The Alpha and Omega, the First and the Last, is your source. He breathed life into you, and He *is* the life that was breathed into you.

Your identity will tell you something about your Maker, and your Maker will tell you what your specifications are.

The limitations of any product you buy are determined by its manufacturer. Microsoft knows what its computers can do; the machines can't do any more than what the programs allow. Toyota cars don't decide how fast they'll go or how fancy they'll look; their makers do. Barbie doesn't pick her wardrobe; Mattel does. Your identity will tell you something about your Maker, and your Maker will tell you what your specifications are.

How fast can you move, child of God? As fast as He'll let you. How much power do you have? Enough power to put your foot on Satan's neck and keep it there. What kind of power do you have? The same power that raised Jesus from the dead. What can you do? You can do all things. How far can you go?

How far is eternity?

6
What the Spirit Says

6
What the Spirit Says

It takes two to speak the truth. One to speak and another to listen.
—*Henry Thoreau*

Sanctify them by Your truth. Your word is truth.
—John 17:17

I want you to get this truth deep into your spirit. If you get this, if you will believe and receive this truth, it will change your life. It will break some yokes that have been hindering your progress. It will shake loose some things that have hanging on to you and your family for generations. This truth will set you free to be blessed, healed, delivered and prospered. It will propel you into the uncommon life!

What is that truth? It's simply this: We're Christians. This means more than what it looks like on the surface. That designation literally means we are "little Christs" or diminutive versions of Christ. Think about it. When we say that we are Christians, we are claiming to be modeled after Jesus. When people look at us, who we are should tell them something about the One we identify ourselves with. That doesn't sound complicated, does it? But it's not as easy to do as it sounds.

God daily transforms us into the image of His Son. That's the simple part of it. However, that transformation takes place at three different levels. God's truth is revealed in us on three different planes. It is molded into what we think. It is made out of what we say. And it is manifested by what we do. In other words, it comes through what we believe, what we say, and what we do. God is constantly working on bringing all three of these facets of our person into agreement with each other and into alignment with Him. You have to understand that or you run the risk of living a common and incomplete life. Notice that I didn't say "Christian life." That's because you can't live like Jesus believing one thing and doing another. You can't claim to be modeled after Him if what you do and what you say don't agree.

When we say we're Christians, we're claiming to be modeled after Jesus.

God, Jesus, and the Holy Spirit are one, and they agree as one. The closest we come to the pattern of that divine trichotomy is in our thoughts, words, and deeds. These three need to line up with God and each other if we are going to truly walk in the truth.

In the previous chapter we dealt primarily with the thought process in the area of knowing our identity. We learned how important it is to identify ourselves with our

Maker. In this and the two chapters following, we're going to look at some of the behaviors or deeds of a person pressing toward the uncommon life. In this chapter we will be looking at the pivotal role of the mouth—ours and God's—in constructing and improving our Christian walk.

Let's get started with Mark 11:22-23.

So Jesus answered and said to them, "Have faith in God. For assuredly, I say to you, whoever says to this mountain, 'Be removed and be cast into the sea,' and does not doubt in his heart, but believes that those things he says will be done, he will have whatever he says."

Now let's go to Romans 4:17.

(As it is written, "I have made you a father of many nations") in the presence of Him whom he believed—God, who gives life to the dead and calls those things which do not exist as though they did.

These are all familiar verses, but I want to reinforce this principle for you. Look next at Hebrews 11:3.

By faith we understand that the worlds were framed by the word of God, so that the things which are seen were not made of things which are visible.

Read these verses over again. When you have time, memorize them, in this order. Then whenever you think about them, tell yourself, "There is a miracle in my mouth."

A Miracle in Your Mouth

Yes, there is a miracle in your mouth! As I read these Scriptures, meditated on them, and digested them, the weight of what they were saying began to settle in my spirit. The words that come out of our mouths are so important. How significant and life-changing are the things we say, whether we whisper or shout them! Those who study the dynamics of communication, particularly interpersonal communication, have understood this principle for a long time. Child rearing experts, behaviorists, and sociologists all agree regarding the power of words to positively or negatively affect the emotional, mental, social, and psychological development of human beings. If you tell a child long enough that he is stupid, for example, you can look for that child to grow up and live out that declaration. Children tend to live up to—or *down* to—whatever your expectations of them are. To paraphrase the writer of Hebrews, their world is framed by the words that have been spoken over them.

How significant and life-changing are the things we say, whether we whisper or shout them!

The power of words to affect our well-being is simply phenomenal. Medical doctors have discovered that patients' recovery and healing can be hastened by a positive attitude. In other words, patients who believed and declared healing got better faster than those who spoke negative things. In fact, some secular studies show that when you speak negative things, your body actually produces hormones and enzymes that adversely affect your health. They can cause you to become depressed, give you headaches, and cause your bones to become dried up. Imagine that! You can actually talk yourself to death if you're not careful. And, as can be expected, the opposite thing happens when you begin to speak good words. Your body responds and improves.

I remember a man who was diagnosed with incurable cancer. Now, this man wasn't a Christian. He didn't know all the biblical principles, but he stumbled onto one: *"A merry heart does good, like medicine"* (Prov. 17:22). This man decided, "Well, if I'm not going to live all that long, I'm at least going to have a good time with what I've got left." So he went out and rented a bunch of Three Stooges movies. He loved laughing at those stooges. So he watched hour upon hour of "Spread out!" and "Woo-woo-woo!" He laughed hysterically at all the eye poking, face slapping, custard pie throwing, and slapstick comedy. This sick man just laughed himself silly.

Some time later he went back to his doctor for a checkup, and the doctor said, "I don't know what you're doing, but something is happening in your body. It's not being taken over by the cancer. It's actually producing something that is fighting it." The fellow didn't have the nerve to tell the doctor what he was doing. He just went back home and watched some more television. He just laughed and carried on every time one of those stooges did something silly. Eventually, the man actually laughed himself back to health.

When you can put on your garment of praise and laugh when there doesn't appear to be a reason to, your body responds. You've got to laugh in the face of danger and when things are going wrong. I'm not talking about some false hilarity. If you let Him, God will show you reasons to rejoice. He can show you how to face every day declaring, *"This is the day the LORD has made; we will rejoice and be glad in it"* (Ps. 118:24). Maybe there are things going on in your life that you don't understand and can't fix. Perhaps there are situations you wish you could change but are beyond your control. Let me tell you something that is not beyond your control: the words of your mouth. You can control your words, and if you will let God guide your tongue, they can control your situation, or at the very least keep your situation from controlling you.

God gave you a mouth, so use it!

Don't allow your mouth to dig a ditch for you. A ditch is not that far from being a grave if you keep talking. Don't frame a prison for yourself with words. When your enemies surround you, use your mouth to shout, "If God be for me, who can be against me? I don't know how, and I don't know when, but I know that God will deliver me. I'm passing through the waters, but He's with me. They won't overtake me. I'm going through the fire, but He is with me. I won't be burned. I won't even smell like smoke!"

Think practically here. Don't get so holy that you think only pious, lovely words have to leave your mouth every time you lift up your voice in your situation. God gave you a mouth, so use it. When the squeeze gets tight, just holler, "Mercy!" if that suits your case. Cry, "Ouch!" if that's how you feel. "Lord!" always works. So much is communicated in that one word. When you cry out, "Lord!" you identify your Savior. You identify *with* your Savior. You acknowledge your Savior's ownership of you. And you humble yourself before your Savior. With just that one word from your lips, you sent up a petition for mercy, comfort, communion, and grace. Any one of those ought to help you with whatever you're going through.

If you observe carefully, you'll find that defeated people use defeated language. Sick people speak with sick language. Poor people speak poor words. Mad folk speak with mad language. Jesus said it this way: *"Out of the abundance of the heart the mouth speaks"* (Matt. 12:34). Every time you speak, you build a framework, a parameter, a fence around your existence. You build a walled city that you have to live in. Jesus said that by the words of your mouth you are justified and by the words of your mouth you are condemned (Matt. 12:37). The Old Testament writer said that life and death are in the power of the tongue (Prov. 18:21).

> *Every time you speak, you build a framework, a parameter, a fence around your existence.*

Let me ask you a question. What is happening in your life today that you are giving life to by the words you speak? Remember, when God created you, He created you in His image. How did God create the world? God spoke it into existence by His word. He quickens the dead and calls things that are not as though they already were (see Romans 4:17 KJV). There is power in the words that you speak. Jesus said if you say to the mountain—not pray to the mountain, but say to it—"be removed," and believe in your heart that what you say will happen, then that mountain will slide right into the sea. Think about that. You have what you say.

Get this principle into your spirit. Take time and examine your life for areas in which you have been speaking death instead of life. You can fall into it very subtly. The devil is always trying to get you to come into agreement with his plan for your destruction, oppression, suppression, depression, possession, and poverty. What are you saying that binds you up and ties you to that plan? Whatever it is, you've got to wash your mouth clean of it. In effect, you've got to wash your mouth out with the truth. That's what Jesus said in John 17. He was asking God to sanctify His disciples: *"Sanctify them by Your truth. Your word is truth"* (v. 17). In other words, He asked God to wash every lie off of and out of them. This goes for us as well. We are His disciples, and we've got to agree with the truth.

Refuse to agree with the devil, your relatives, your friends, your teacher, or anybody else who doesn't believe that you are fearfully and wonderfully made. Refuse to agree with them, and then put some word in your mouth to prepare for the next time you have to address the issue. You are who God says you are— nothing more, and certainly nothing less. You can have what God says you can have, and you can do whatever He says you can do.

You are who God says you are—nothing more, and certainly nothing less.

You've got to come to the place where you say only what God says over your life. Do you realize that generational curses are carried on the lips of mothers, fathers, aunts, uncles, grandparents, cousins, brothers, and sisters who are themselves prisoners of tradition, unforgiveness, lies, and secrets? Most of us grow up in families where things have been done a certain way for so long that we just assume they are normal, until we check out somebody else's family or become a member of the household of faith. Until you realize that "normal" is only what God says is normal, you can never be delivered from the generational strongholds in your family that bind you.

It is very easy for someone who is bound by particular strongholds and spirits to release those things into the next generation through socializa-tion and accepted lifestyles. Then those strongholds are reinforced by the words that come out of the mouths of the authority figures in people's lives. We are taught all kinds of things through words, and we don't realize the power they have over us until we try to set ourselves free.

If you want to reorder your world, then you're going to have to reorder your words.

Think about the "death words" that we say all the time, like "That scared me to death." We live in a culture of death. It's all around us. But if you want to reorder your world, then you're going to have to reorder your words. I remem-ber when I got saved, and I remember specifically when I started getting revelation and understanding on how to live in victory. One of the first areas that God really began to challenge me on were the words that were coming out of my mouth. You simply cannot get free, be successful, and live an abundant life as long as you keep talking yourself into fear, defeat, and failure.

Has the Holy Spirit ever put a check on your mouth? He did it to me. Every time I would say something that wasn't in line with the will of God, the Holy Spirit would say, "Wait, wait, wait. What are you saying? You're going to have what you say." He was working on some of the other pastors at the church at the same time He was working on me. So we would start to check each other. Somebody would say something, and we'd say to that person, "Hmm. You're going to have what you say." Of course, when this all started, we didn't always do things in the right spirit. For a while we were like the word police. You couldn't say anything negative around us. We sort of got sick of ourselves after a while. But, it did make us think about the words that came out of our mouths.

Please, don't get out of balance with this. I'm not suggesting that you can just pick anything you want and, if you click your heels together and say it long enough, it will happen. I'm not talking about that; I'm talking about what is attached to belief in your heart. God has given you the power to speak what you believe into existence. But, it has to be what He has already put in your spirit. As with all things, it begins with Him, and it's according to His will.

God has given you the power to speak what you believe into existence.

God will quicken, or make alive, the dead. He calls those things that are not as though they already were. He speaks life. Think for a few minutes about how many times you agree with the enemy rather than with God. We know that the devil came to kill, steal, and destroy, and that Jesus came to give us an abundant life of healthiness, holiness, and happiness (John 10:10). We understand that, but still many of our words are in agreement with what the enemy wants to do in our lives, and not what God wants to do.

Death words, sick words, poor words—they all build a framework around us that entrap us if we're not careful. Actually, what happens is those words build a reality around us that wouldn't even exist if it weren't for those words and our refusal to disagree with them. We know, for example, that the economy, even in our nation, has a lot to do with confidence. It doesn't even have as much to do with actual numbers as it has to do with our confidence in those numbers. If somebody gets on television and starts talking fear and recession, pretty soon we end up in one. But if someone starts talking about increase and expansion, we end up there. Many times it's all because of our confidence level. Those words have an impact on our spending, saving, and buying habits.

> *Jesus said that you can't change anything by worrying about it, so why worry?*

So often people get into the practice of speaking words of despair and doubt. Check your conversation. Are you speaking despair and doubt? "I don't know what I'm going to do." "I don't know what's going to become of me." "How are we going to make it?" That's worry, fear, and the spirit of fear. Some of us are always fearful, always afraid, and always worried. Why? Look at what's being said. "I'm just worried to death about so-and-so." Do you know something? That person is going to be fine and living, but you're going to be dead from worrying! Jesus Himself said that you can't change anything by worrying about it, so why worry? (Read Matthew 6.)

People say things like, "I can't afford to tithe." What kind of confession is that? The truth is, you can't afford not to tithe! When you don't tithe, you come into agreement with the enemy who is stealing, killing, and destroying your finances. That's no testimony to the goodness of God.

Framed into Reality

Sometimes spiritual, relational, and psychological things combine to build a frame around our lives that words help solidify or hold in place. Imagine a picture frame. It is not the picture, but it is the thing surrounding the picture that makes it look a certain way. Sometimes people are drawn into generational curses—into agreement with the plan of the enemy for their lives—because of the way things are presented to them. Sometimes a negative thought can be framed in a positive light, and therefore you receive it because you feel you'll get some benefit from it.

Think about it this way. Suppose you find out that there is a spirit of infirmity in a certain family. I'm not talking about just one person getting a cold every now and then. I'm talking about a spirit, where the same thing happens generation after generation. There's always somebody sick. There's always somebody weak and frail. Then you find out, after a little investigation, that people in that family get expressions of love and sympathy and attention whenever they are sick. They get coddled and waited on. It wouldn't take a three-year-old very long to find out that when he gets sick, he gets soup and nice presents. People who haven't seen you for a while come by to visit you. They hold your hand, pat you on the head, and say, "Baby, everything is going to be okay." You get attention that you don't get when you're healthy. When you're healthy, everybody looks over you and goes on about their business. So it doesn't take long, if there's a spirit of infirmity working, for you to figure out that being sick is not such a bad deal. You don't have as much work when you're sick. There's not as much pressure when you're sick. There's more attention when you're sick. You get gifts when you don't feel well.

Pretty soon you're saying, "I'm a little weak today." "I feel dizzy." "Feel my forehead. Do I have a fever?" "I don't feel well. I can't do this. I can't do that." Whenever you need a little attention, you start to feel a little under the weather. Eventually, all that speaking begins to convince you. That's how hypochondriacs are born. You've got every kind of pill in every shape and color, and you just can't seem to get better. Do you know why? You probably don't want to.

What you say about yourself solidifies your reality.

It is possible to know intellectually that you should want to be better, but emotionally not be able to let go of that spirit because you don't want to live without all the attention. Your head is telling you that you should be getting better, but your heart doesn't really want to because you have developed an identity around being sick. Your relationships are most alive when you are sick. You feel the most valuable and the most valued when you are sick. As twisted as it sounds, you feel your best when you are sick. So you build your reality around sickness. As a result, what you say about yourself solidifies your reality.

I have talked to many health care professionals, and they all say the same thing. The emergency rooms are usually more full of "regulars" than new people. The same folks are in and out of there all the time. Doctors know them by name. Nurses have a room for them. It's always something.

There are some families that are so dysfunctional that they come together only when there's a tragedy. They don't even see each other unless somebody is sick or dead. Families like that are tough to get old in. There are seniors in apartments and rest homes who get phone calls or letters only when one of their children has passed on or been hurt. Only then do kids, grandkids, nephews and nieces all come together, bake pies, hold hands, and pray—and pretend that it's closeness.

Nothing is beyond God's power to make new.

In a family like that, words—the ones thrown carelessly around with no real relationship to support—become a framework of lies that block us from intimate, honest contact, and that wall gets harder to penetrate after time has cemented it. At that point "I love you" doesn't really mean anything. "I'll call you" carries the same weight as "Take out the trash." "How are you?" is simply a rhetorical question. Nobody's really looking for an answer to it. Each time words are spoken in an environment like that, another rip is made in the fabric of the family. Soon, it appears to be torn beyond repair. Notice it *appears* to be.

One of the things I love about God is that nothing is beyond His power to heal. Nothing is beyond His power to make new. All He needs is one person willing to speak life into that dead situation. You see, we don't serve a God who can just help us deal with death; our God overcomes death with life.

Watch what happens if just one person decides to express love and not ambivalence. Go ahead. Your family will be a thousand times better than it is—even if it's already great—if you purpose to speak more life into it.

Speak Blessings

You are what you say. You are also what you think. If you think poverty, you will have poverty. Poverty thinking produces poverty actions. Sometimes poor thinking and poor speaking concern more than just economics. Being broke is a temporary economic condition, but poverty is a spirit. It's a mentality. It's

Being broke is a temporary economic condition, but poverty is a spirit.

a stronghold that won't let you get up and out. Some people are so bound up by these spirits that they will even begin to speak over your life words that can come back to haunt you later.

Many times words are spoken over people—really against people—who have more than you have. Those words plant seeds in you, telling you that if you ever get to have more too, the people closest to you won't like you. If you were raised around people who said things like, "She thinks she's this or that because she's got money," or "He might be living in that big house, but I wouldn't trade places with him." If you were raised by envious, covetous people who couldn't stand to see anybody with more than they had, they might have given you the impression that having nice things is wrong or evil. Without realizing it, parents, some of your jealousy and envy could be the very thing holding your children back from becoming successful. Deep down they may feel like you won't accept them if they do better than you, so they try to sabotage their own success. They may feel guilty about being blessed financially.

That kind of guilt is the reason some of you have to explain yourselves every time God blesses you. You can't have anything nice without telling somebody that you got a good deal on it. That's not necessarily their business. Now, that doesn't mean you can't share good deals with others. It means you ought not excuse God's goodness for the sake of someone else's opinion.

I've had to deal with this issue. Sometimes people give me things, and I have to deal with the feeling that I wouldn't want someone to think that I just went out and bought those things and was wasteful. A lot of pastors go through this. Even though the item is a gift, I think that people might make assumptions about things they don't know about. So when somebody makes a comment like, "Oh, that's a nice whatever," I feel obliged to tell them, "Well, you know, somebody gave this to me. I didn't buy it." Or, "I got that on sale."

We need to ask ourselves—I know I do—"Am I doing all that explaining because I feel guilty about being blessed? Do I have to expound and make excuses because I don't want someone to think about me a certain way?" If somebody can't handle your being blessed, then you're probably wasting your energy explaining anyway. Such people will walk away and say what they're going to say anyway. We have to decide that we're going to quit wasting our words on our guilt and start using them to bless the Lord and praise Him for all that He has done and is doing in our lives.

I also believe that poverty thinking and poverty speaking have more to do with values than the actual cost of things. A poverty mentality will place a false light on the value of things, and that is what will keep you down. For example, a person may be in an impoverished situation. There's no screen door on the house; the address numbers are falling off. Yet, there's a nice car parked outside. That person may have some money coming in some kind of way, so he decided to take the money and put some new rims on the car instead of getting a screen for the front door. You can see that the issue is not about money. It's about a value system. It doesn't make sense to spend a hundred dollars on a pair of sneakers if you don't have a winter coat. It's not a money issue; it's a values issue.

Quit wasting your words on guilt and start using them to bless the Lord.

People with a poverty mentality typically rack up all kinds of credit card debt. Why? It's about values. What is more important? Ownership now and pay later, or save now and own later?

Simply put, running up debt—especially credit card debt—is borrowing against your future. You don't value your future if you're willing to consume it before you reach it. The Bible says a wise man leaves an inheritance for his children and his children's children (Prov. 13:22). When the family focuses on satisfying today's appetite and eating the seed that would bring a harvest tomorrow, it teaches the children that they don't have any value. That's a poverty culture.

Your children should see you save, even if you have to go without in order to do it. They should see you tithe and put money away for your retirement and their college tuition. They can learn to go without a new bike today if it means that you can bless somebody who has a financial need. We spend so much time teaching our children how to get, buy, and consume. How much time do we spend teaching them how to give, save, and spend wisely? When we allow a poverty mentality to pervade our homes, we're building a framework for our children's lives that may keep them in bondage for years to come.

To top that off, words of sickness, defeat, worry, and tragedy are spoken. We're always down. We can't do this. We mustn't do that. And next thing you know, you come into agreement with the lie of the enemy. You start living the life that you've built around you.

The Bible says that God *"gives life to the dead and calls those things which do not exist as though they did"* (Rom. 4:17). That doesn't mean lie. Rather, God can see what's coming, and He just calls it out before it takes place so that when the blessing comes, you'll know it's from Him. He calls the things that are not as though they already were. He does not call the things that are as though they are not.

God makes the dead alive because, to God, death is merely what happens before resurrection. It doesn't bother Him. In fact, He uses death to prove His power in our lives. That passage in Romans 4 talks about Abraham and how God called him *"the father of many nations"* before he had any kids. God called those things that were not as though they already were. God didn't wait for Abraham to have kids before He called him a father. He didn't have to. God already knew what was going to take place in Abraham's life.

Let me give you a word of caution here. Make sure you let God tell you what to speak over someone's life. Don't get careless with your mouth; you could do some serious damage. Don't spank your kid because he told a lie, and then while you're spanking him call him a liar. "I'm spanking you because you're a liar!" Don't do that. You're trying to keep him from lying, not beat that reality into him. You should be disciplining him because he's *not* a liar, and he told a lie. When you're spanking your child for telling a lie, it should be to let him know that you know he's not a liar, and he is being punished for acting contrary to the truth about himself. If you're disciplining that child and saying, "You're a liar! You're a liar! You're a liar!" you're speaking that over him, and when he becomes a lying teenager and eventually a lying adult, you're going to have to shoulder some of the blame for that.

> *To God, death is merely what happens before resurrection.*

You will have whatever you say. Whatever you say, you will have. Let's look at one more verse before we close this chapter. This issue of the mouth is very real and very important. Everybody has to review his life in this area from time to time. We all could use some help in this area.

Now, please don't get legalistic about this. You don't need to go to extremes where you can't take a joke or have fun. Everything doesn't have to be overly serious. What we're concerned with here is what you believe and what you say because of what you believe. What's coming out of your mouth? What are you speaking over your family? What are you speaking over your finances? What are you saying about who you are?

Sister, what are you saying about your beauty? It's not enough to say with your mouth that you are fearfully and wonderfully made if you don't believe it in your heart. If you say it without believing it, you're speaking lies over yourself. Wash your mouth with the truth of God's Word. Get to the place where you don't just say you are fearfully and wonderfully made, but you'll add, like David did, that your soul knows that fact for sure.

Stop agreeing with death and hell.

Now, look at Isaiah 28:18: *"Your covenant with death will be annulled, and your agreement with Sheol* [hell] *will not stand."*

Make a decision to stop agreeing with death and hell. Break your contract with them. You do that by refusing to seal the lie of the enemy with the words of your mouth. Most of us—not all, but most—grew up in homes where people didn't pay much attention to what was spoken over and into the members who lived there. That doesn't make us evil. It doesn't mean anything is wrong with our families. It just means that the devil has assignments standing against you that you might not know about. Some of those assignments are being carried out in the words that were uttered in the home you grew up in. Those words have built a framework that actually facilitates the movement of the spirits assigned to hinder you. Satan will do everything he can to keep you from accomplishing God's will in your life. He'll try to get you addicted, in poverty, depressed, angry, jealous, or sick. He may be weaving a web of racism and prejudice around you and in you, or one that encourages adultery and infidelity. He could be chipping away at your self-esteem to continue a cycle of abuse in your family. Whatever the enemy's assignment is, cancel it.

Stop agreeing with the death assignments that have been placed over your life. Stop renewing your covenant with hell. Jesus told us how:

> *Whatever the enemy's assignment is, cancel it.*

Again I say to you that if two of you agree on earth concerning anything that they ask, it will be done for them by My Father in heaven. (Matt. 18:19)

You've got to quit talking defeat. You've got to quit talking fear. It won't make sense to you at first, but you'll soon get the hang of it. Agree with God and with the people of God and stop agreeing with the devil and the people he's using to do his dirty work.

Start calling those things that are not as though they already are. I don't mean just plucking wishes out of the air and reciting them. Ask God to open up His mouth and speak into your life, in prayer, through His Word, and through trusted vessels. I promise that what He will tell you will always be greater than what you already have. Then start speaking those things over your life and over the lives of the people you love.

There is a miracle in your mouth. That miracle is the Word of God. By it the worlds were framed. By it your world is waiting to be framed. Make a new contract with a Divine Architect. Let Him tell you everything you ever wanted to hear about love, wealth, purpose, vision, relationships, and abundant life. Then repeat what He says and watch your miracle take shape!

7
A Time for War

7
A Time for War

---◆◆◆---

The devil takes no holiday; he never rests. If beaten, he rises again.
If he cannot enter in front, he steals in the rear. If he cannot enter at
the rear, he breaks through the roof or enters by tunneling under the
threshold. He labors until he is in. He uses great cunning and many
a plan. When one miscarries, he has another at hand and continues
his attempts until he wins.
—Ewald M. Plass

But let us who are of the day be sober, putting on the
breastplate of faith and love, and as a helmet the hope
of salvation.
—1 Thessalonians 5:8

One day I was looking through some notes of things I had taught at my church, and I came across something that I had talked about as it related to spiritual attacks in people's lives. What struck me was that it was dated some time ago. I hadn't addressed the subject with my congregation in years, yet I was sure most of them had encountered some form of spiritual attack during the intervening time. If they hadn't, then they were most assuredly due for one!

I have found that when it comes to this issue of spiritual battles, all the people of God fall into one of three categories: They are in a fight with the devil; they have just come out of a fight with the devil; or they are on their way into a fight with the devil. He never leaves us alone. When Jesus defeated him in the wilderness, the Word says that Satan departed from him *"for a season"* (Luke 4:13 KJV). Now, if the devil is crazy enough to take on Jesus, then surely those of us who are Jesus' disciples are on his hit list as well.

You cannot live your life as a child of the kingdom and never encounter the enemy.

Paul and Peter were very clear on the matter. The devil is looking for a fight 24 hours a day, 7 days a week, 365 days a year. His goal is not just to take down God's people, but to take them out. So in case you have not discovered this fact yet, let me tell you: You cannot live your life as a child of the kingdom and never encounter the enemy. If you haven't crossed his path or locked horns with him yet, keep living. He's on his way.

So what do we do? Ephesians 6 tells us to expect attacks and be ready to fight.

> *Finally, my brethren, be strong in the Lord and in the power of His might. Put on the whole armor of God, that you may be able to stand against the wiles of the devil. For we do not wrestle against flesh and blood, but against*

principalities, against powers, against the rulers of the darkness of this age, against spiritual hosts of wickedness in the heavenly places. Therefore take up the whole armor of God, that you may be able to withstand in the evil day, and having done all, to stand. (Eph. 6:10–13)

The Bible is clear as it relates to us that all God's people—not just a few—must enter and endure seasons of conflict, seasons of attack, and seasons of intense internal and external pressure in their lives. Sometimes these seasons occur as natural events that work against you, and such are common to all men. (See 1 Corinthians 10:13.) There are certain things that just happen to everyone who lives on this planet. The fact that you are a Christian does not mean that you escape all hardship, pain, or adversity. It doesn't mean that everyone in your family is going to live forever. It doesn't mean that it will never rain on your parade. Stuff happens, to believers and unbelievers alike, simply because we live in this world.

Stuff happens, to believers and unbelievers alike, simply because we live in this world.

Then there are other things that are not so natural or common—things that are more spiritual in nature. The Bible teaches that our adversary is the devil, who is spirit. First Peter 5:8–9 tells us,

Be sober, be vigilant; because your adversary the devil walks about like a roaring lion, seeking whom he may devour. Resist him, steadfast in the faith, knowing that the same sufferings are experienced by your brotherhood in the world.

We know that this adversary, the enemy of our souls, is diligent and vicious. He's never late. He's up every morning. In fact, he's waiting on you to get out of bed. He's ever watching over his prey. He's never tardy. He never calls in sick. He's always working to bring about destruction in the life of every believer. If you're a believer, then make no mistake; the devil is your adversary.

The response we should make to him is not always easy to do, but it is not complicated at all. We're to resist him, period. Now that word *resist* does not mean to merely ignore. It doesn't mean to just walk away from. That word is actually a military term that means to actively work against. So if you will resist the devil, if you will take active steps against him, he will flee from you.

> *The enemy is diligent and vicious. The response we should make isn't always easy, but it's not complicated.*

Notice also that this passage says he is *"seeking"* whom he may devour. That tells us that there are those whom he may devour and those whom he may not devour. Now, the enemy knows which saints he can devour. He has had many centuries to develop a keen capacity to judge human nature. He cannot read your mind, but he can know what's inside your mind when it comes out of your mouth. That's why you have to guard what you say, even in times of hurt and conflict, when you're tired or upset and angry, or when you don't feel like you have the victory. It is even more important to keep confessing the victory in those times because the enemy cannot read your mind.

The devil is a past master at reading our body language and reading the way that we respond to situations. He pays close attention to the way we are moved or not moved by things, and he measures our emotions, our mood swings, and our reactions to things that happen in our lives. He is an expert on human behavior.

I'm saying all this to give you some understanding. God's people can be ignorant about the enemy's devices. We can be so bold that we're foolish. The devil is defeated, yes, but he is not stupid. On the contrary, he is skilled at finding every weakness in a person, a family, or a nation, and exploiting that weakness to the fullest. Yes, he can judge very quickly by your behavior and your responses if you're one of those he can devour or if he needs to go on to somebody else.

> *The devil is defeated, but he's not stupid. On the contrary, he's an expert on human behavior.*

My purpose in this chapter is to make you, in one sense, "devil-proof," so that even when he does attack you—and he will—he will not accomplish his intended goal. The Bible exhorts us to put on the whole armor of God and to understand that each piece has a purpose and a function. If we don't have on the whole armor, if we miss a piece, then parts of us will be more vulnerable to attack.

So many have walked with God long enough to know, in theory and through experience, that it's possible for a believer to be fortified in one area and yet open to attack in another. It's possible for you to have great faith for physical healing and yet not exercise information or faith as it relates to your finances, and vice versa. It's possible to have great faith when it relates to spiritual things and not know how to exercise your faith as it relates to practical matters like employment, family relationships, or peace of mind. Friend, let's put on the whole armor of God so that we can stand against all the cunning devices of the devil.

Get Ready for Attacks

The Scriptures tell us that when the children of Israel came out of Egypt, Pharaoh sent *"chosen chariots"* after them (Exod. 14:7 KJV). He didn't send just any chariots; he sent specific ones, the ones specially designed for war. The devil works the same way.

When you look at the context of Isaiah 54:17, you'll find something interesting. That verse says, *"No weapon formed against you shall prosper."* When it talks about the weapon that is formed, it does not mean an indiscriminate weapon. It is, in actuality, something that is specifically designed to attack a specific weak spot in your life. It does not speak of an enemy just picking up a weapon and chucking it in your general direction. It's talking about a weapon that was designed after a flaw was discovered, one that was expressly purposed to take you out at the point of that frailty. It is a device formed and fashioned to fit your specific vulnerability. You, the target, were in the mind of your enemy as he made the weapon. That means that he has studied you. He has studied your family. He has studied your environment. He has studied you from a child, and it was at that point that he began to prepare devices against you.

That's the bad news. The good news is that while he's been studying you, God has already studied him. One of the enemy's failings is that he's not creative. He hasn't come up with any new tricks since he was cast out of heaven. He is still a deceiver. He is still a liar. He is still an accuser. So God says, "I've given to you My whole armor so that you can stand against him." The armor hasn't changed because Satan hasn't changed, and the fact that God is in control of every situation hasn't changed either.

If you have on the whole armor of God, then even in the days of your greatest attack you will outlast your enemy. The evidence of a Christian life is not the absence of storms, the absence of attacks, or the absence of pressures that come against you. Rather, it is the ability to stand strong and win the victory over those things. Jesus talked about two houses built by two different men, one upon the rock and the other upon the sand. Those houses represent our Christian life. Each endured wind, rain, and floodwaters that beat violently against it. So the evidence of your position in Christ is not whether or not you have a storm. The evidence of your faith is not in your ability to avoid the storm. The evidence of your faith is whether or not you're still standing when the storm is over.

While the devil has been studying you, God has already studied him.

When you look at it that way, the storm does not come to harm you. Instead, the storm comes to validate your faith and to show those around you who have no faith the power of faith. The fact that you're still standing when it's all over tells the world that you are built on something that is worth them building their lives on. So when you go through the hardships of life and come out on the other side no worse for the wear; when you come out on the other side still standing, your praise still intact, your head still up, your smile still in place, and a spring still in your step, then it becomes a testimony to people that they ought to consider what they're standing on.

I am convinced that no one who comes to the altar and makes a commitment to Christ is easily released by the devil. He's going to put up a fight to keep that person. Sooner or later, that individual will face his first opposition to his faith. I see and I know by experience and through the Word of God that every person comes to places of testing and challenge in his life. As a pastor I get concerned and pray that people's faith won't fail because there are certain

The evidence of your faith is whether or not you're still standing when the storm is over.

things that no one can protect you from. There are certain things that everyone has to find for him or herself. For example, every person will come to the place where he wants to give up. If you show me a person who has never wanted to give up, I'll show you a person who hasn't been saved for very long. Wanting to give up is a crisis that comes to every Christian. It crosses every mind and heart.

Everyone will be, at some time in his life, offended. Yes, everyone. The first time somebody offends you is one of your greatest tests in Christian faith. And if somebody close to you offends you, it's even harder to handle. Nevertheless, it is a part of your life as a believer. Jesus said, *"Offenses must come"* (Matt. 18:7). I have been around people whose main "anointing" was to be an offense. They knew how to stir it up and how to dwell on it and in it.

I have learned that the less committed to his faith a person is, the more easily he is offended. People in churches all across America leave their church over an offense, only to return years later. They give up on God simply because they were offended by something somebody said or something they didn't like. Perhaps somebody didn't shake their hands one Sunday. Maybe they were released from a ministry position. Or they wanted to sing a solo in the choir and didn't get to. So they got offended, got their feelings hurt, and gave up on God. It all sounds silly, doesn't it? It is silly. But it happens, and we all know that it happens. People get attached emotionally to trivial things, which makes you wonder if their commitment to God was also trivial and small. But, when you get to the place where you are able to deal with offense properly, process it, get over it, and get on with life, then you have crossed one of your first major hurdles in your relationship with God.

People give up on God because they were offended by something a person did.

Another hurdle in your Christianity appears the first time you don't get your prayer answered right away. The enemy loves to attack you at this point. When this happens, he can hit you with lies and accusations as well as fear and uncertainty.

When you're first born again, it seems like there's such favor on your life. And there is, really. It seems like before you can even pray a prayer, the answer is on the way.

What is really happening is that God is moving beyond your theological knowledge (actually your lack thereof). He moves beyond your correctness and verbiage because it seems like you need something. You think you need stuff, but He knows you need confidence to approach Him boldly. So He shows you unusually prompt responses to your petitions. You just think it, and there it is. You walk around thinking, "My Lord, where've You been all these years? God is taking care of me."

Sooner or later, though, you will ask God for something and He will turn you down or tell you to wait. One time when I said that, a person struggling with this issue replied,

Sooner or later, you're going to ask God for something and He'll say no or tell you to wait.

"No, no, pastor. I get everything I want from God." That person didn't want to hear that. "Well," I said, "the Bible says sometimes you have not because you ask amiss. Perhaps you're asking out of the will of God." Have you ever asked for something that wasn't in the will of God? You're not going to receive some of the things you're praying for if they're outside the will of God for your life. I know it's not comfortable to hear that, but it's right.

You are going to pray for some people who are not going to get better. Some people don't like to hear that, either. One time I was invited to teach at a Bible school. The ministers there had done a wonderful job of teaching and inspiring faith in the hearts of all the young Bible school students. They had talked about how they gave away a car, how the people they prayed for got healed of cancer, and about going to cities and shaking them up with the Gospel.

They had done that for a number of weeks, and the young people were all pumped up and ready to take the world for God. Then they asked me to come and speak. I said, "Well, I'm going to tell the other side of that coin, just so you don't get out there and fall apart."

Please don't misunderstand me. I have faith for people to be healed. I believe we're supposed to lay hands on the sick, as Scripture says. But I also have prayed for people who died. (You might be thinking, "Don't call Pastor Pitts if I get sick.") I don't always understand why people die anyway when I have prayed fervently and earnestly for them. But you see, my faith is not based on my ability to understand the secret things that belong to the Lord.

I know what my job is when I walk into a hospital room. My job is to pray the prayer of faith. My job is to lay hands on the patient. My job is to decree the Word of the Lord. However, you can't make anybody be anything, and if you live long enough, you'll learn that some people you pray for simply won't get better. I'm telling you this to keep you from having a shipwreck in your faith. Why? Some people, the first time they pray for somebody who doesn't get better, will just give up on God.

Just because you got saved doesn't mean it's going to rain hundred-dollar bills on your head every day. Everyone has hurdles to face. You have to come to the point where those things don't move your faith away from God. You don't let them stop you from praying for the sick, believing in prosperity, or trusting in miracles. You don't believe the lies of the enemy. You just keep on standing and say, "These things belong to the Lord, and some of them I'll understand by and by."

There are many things that you aren't going to understand. I don't say that to put doubt in your heart, but so you'll understand how to stand. You're not going to get everything that you ask for. Everybody you pray for is not going to get better. You are going to run into some hard times and you are going to be offended at some point in your life. These are facts, and if you don't understand that these things are coming, they will surprise you. And when you're surprised, the enemy uses it as leverage against you and begins to challenge your faith.

It is absolutely true that the life of a Christian is a victorious life. It's a prosperous life and a healthy life. But in the midst of hardship, my faith is not based on whether God ever gives me a car or whether everybody I touch gets healed. My faith is based on nothing less than Jesus' blood and His righteousness. If God doesn't ever do anything else for me, I'm going to serve Him anyway. People can act silly and try to offend me. They might make me mad, but I won't let it get down in my spirit. I won't let it become a root of bitterness. I'm just going to throw it off and let God deal with it and them. But I'm not going to claim my right to anger and lose my crown.

My faith is based on nothing less than Jesus' blood and His righteousness.

Resist the devil and he will flee. Fight him with the sword of the Spirit, which is the Word of God. The Word says to love those who hate you and pray for those who treat you badly (Matt. 5:44). You've got to remember that the fight is never horizontal. We do not fight against flesh and blood. People are never your problem. The devil is not trying to stir up conflict between you and people; he's trying to sever the relationship between you and God. You're not fighting to stay friends with people. You're fighting to stay next to God. That's a fight I don't plan to lose. The devil also designs seasons of attack right at the point where you're about to break through to a new level with God. But, the genius of God is that He will use that attack to push you right over into that new level.

You have to understand that the enemy sees your anointing. He sees your gifting and your talent. He sees your potential more than you do and many times more than the people around you do. At the same time, he also sees the evidence and signs of breakthrough. Thus, so many times, just before breakthrough, an attack is launched against you to keep you from getting to your breakthrough. Don't get discouraged by this, though; instead, when you see an attack, just shout! Get that wild Holy Spirit faith that says, "My Lord, if I'm under attack, then something big is getting ready to happen! Devil, you just gave yourself away. You wouldn't be fighting me so hard if I didn't have something coming to me from heaven!"

The devil wants to sever the relationship between you and God.

I have discovered that people tend to act up just before their moment of breakthrough. For instance, you would have no idea that some people will ever serve God just before they get saved. They say, "I'm never going to serve God," and just get uglier and meaner. They dig their feet into the ground. They go on a three-week drug binge. They wreck their car. They get deep in debt. All the time, their moment is coming. The devil is a liar because God said, "If they're Mine, they're Mine!" People can act up all they want to, but the Word of the Lord shall stand!

You see, that car wreck put them in the hospital and almost killed them. Now they're scared straight. They hobble into church the first Sunday after they get released from the hospital. Or that debt landed them in jail, and now they've got nothing to do but stay out of trouble and read the Bible their mother sent to them in the mail.

I said all that to say this. You cannot be moved by what people do. Just recognize that the meaner

When the devil attacks, God is up to something.

they act, the more the Holy Spirit is working on them and they can't get any peace. God is wrestling with them, and He's not going to stop wrestling 'til the breaking of a new day.

So when you see an attack coming, just get ready, excited, and happy. James said to *"count it all joy"* (James 1:2). Peter said not to let it throw you (1 Pet. 4:12). Jesus said it is par for the course (Matt. 18:7). Paul said to press through it (Phil. 3:12). John said not to love your life unto death (Rev. 12:11). I'm telling you, when the devil is coming down on you, *rest* assured, because God is up to something.

Ten Signs of Spiritual Attack

As a pastor, I have the unique opportunity to see a lot of things take place within a large group of people. Over the years I have watched and advised as people learn to navigate the sometimes choppy waters of the Christian life. As a result of watching different patterns emerge, I have discovered ten signs that indicate a person may be under spiritual attack.

Let me interject here that I don't believe that everything in life is an attack. Some people think that every time anything happens, they are under attack. If they get a flat tire, then the devil is after their car. Or they think they've got a "bill demon" in their mailbox because every time they go to get the mail, there's a new bill in there. That sort of thing.

Of course, other people don't think that anything is an attack. These people walk around in total denial while everything around them is falling apart. Everything is crashing down around them, and they don't believe that they are under attack. They'd rather believe that the problem is something they can fix or control. An attack would take matters out of their hands and force them to trust God for the outcome. God, however, has a way of applying just enough pressure to squeeze an "Uncle!" out of you. Or in His case, it would be "Father!"

#1 —Loss of Spiritual Desire

I don't know a lot about the medical profession, but I do know that one sign of sickness is a loss of appetite. In the same way, one of the first signs of being under spiritual attack is a loss of spiritual appetite.

The Bible teaches us that we are to desire the sincere milk of the Word of God as newborn babes (1 Pet. 2:2). Scripture is filled with terms that refer to our desire and our relationship toward God that indicate that it ought not be perfunctory, or matter-of-fact, or academic, but filled with passion. *"As the deer pants for the water brooks, so pants my soul for You, O God"* (Ps. 42:1). There is a desire and a seeking and a passion that relates to our relationship with God. I want you to see the difference, because it's possible for you to do all the right things and yet have no passion or desire attached to them. You can be doing the right thing and be passionless the whole time you're doing it.

The Bible doesn't say that God loves givers. It says that He loves a *"cheerful giver"* (2 Cor. 9:7). It's possible for you to be giving your tithes and be mad about it. You can lose your desire to give. You're still giving because you're afraid of being cursed, but you don't have a desire to give. You're still praying because you're in trouble, but you don't have a desire to pray. Eventually you start coming up with excuses for not going to church. Your lack of desire regarding these things is an indication that you are under attack.

> *You can be doing the right thing and be passionless the whole time you're doing it.*

#2 — Physical Fatigue

Oftentimes when the enemy attacks someone, he will begin by trying to wear them down physically. A lot of studies talk about the ill effects of stress on the body. When you become stressed out, your body begins to work overtime just to keep you moving. Let's be practical here. When you're worn out, you're weak and not alert. That's the best time for Satan to defeat you. You've got to be careful that you don't put yourself in a vulnerable position.

#3 — *Lack Attack*

A third sign that you're under attack is what I call a "lack attack." In other words, your resources begin to dry up. Again, this lack is not a result of careless spending. In this attack, the goal of the enemy is to get your eyes off of God and your eyes on money. Why? If you're not careful and you hit a cash crunch, if you've got more month than money and things begin to dry up, then you could be tricked into putting your eyes on money and taking them off God. You will think that money is your answer rather than understanding that Jesus is your answer.

Money or God—whichever one you put your focus on is the one that you think is your source. When you start to look to money as your source, you will begin to do things that actually further your demise—and all the time you're convinced that you're helping yourself. For example, if you begin to tell yourself that it's more important for you to get in a few hours of overtime on Sunday than it is to go to church, you've taken your eyes off God and helped the enemy get you further away from the only answer to your problem.

> *Money or God—the one you focus on is the one you think is your source.*

You might excuse yourself by saying it's only for one week, but one week can easily turn into two weeks. After two weeks, all of a sudden it's a month. And so it goes until you start to feel out of sorts and the devil starts to condemn you for staying away so long and makes you too ashamed to go back.

You have to be careful. It's not worth it to get your eyes on money and then start making decisions in your life based on opportunity rather than revelation. God is not the only one who will try to open up a door in your life. Every "opportunity" is not from God. Keep your eyes on Him.

#4 — Prayer Attack

A prayer attack is evident when, every time you go to pray, something happens. Have you ever gone through those seasons in your life where you're trying to pray, and, first of all, you're not feeling the way you want to? Don't let feelings stop you, because prayer is not an unction; it is a discipline. It doesn't require feelings to be effective. It just requires commitment. It's good when there's an unction to pray. You can stir up an unction. But there also are times when you pray just because you are supposed to pray.

Prayer is not an unction; it's a discipline.

When you are under a prayer attack, it seems like there's no joy in it, there's no flow in it, or there's no time for it, because something always happens. The phone rings, the kids break something, the cat eats the goldfish, someone knocks on the door, something burns in the oven, there's a car wreck out in front of your house—something. Every time you go to pray, something happens. You get down on your knees to pray, and your mind is thinking about everything but God.

Even the disciples fell victim to a prayer attack. In Matthew 26 Jesus took Peter and some others to a place called Gethsemane and told them, "You stay here, and I'm going to go pray." He told them to pray so that they would not enter into temptation. He knew that the spirit of man was willing, but his flesh weak. What did the disciples do? They all fell asleep. Prayer attack.

#5—Feeling Overwhelmed

Another sign that you are under attack is when you start feeling overwhelmed. When you're not under attack, you're able to handle different circumstances, scenarios, and situations with a certain amount of confidence and optimism. You believe that things in general will work out and that somehow you will get through it. You may not be able to figure it all out, but you're going to keep plodding away and you don't allow it to get the best of you. However, when you get too far under an attack, you start feel-

> *When you're under attack, it's hard to believe that all things work together for good.*

ing overwhelmed when those circumstances, scenarios, and situations crop up. You start feeling like there's no light at the end of the tunnel. You start getting that "what's the use" attitude. You start feeling like your problems are showing up in groups of three. About the time you get one dealt with, you've got two more to deal with.

The purpose of this attack is to wear you down, to make you tired, and to make you feel hopeless. David gave us a solution. He said, *"I cry out to the LORD with my voice; with my voice to the LORD I make my supplication. I pour out my complaint before Him; I declare before Him my trouble. When my spirit was overwhelmed within me, then You knew my path. In the way in which I walk they have secretly set a snare for me"* (Ps. 142:1–3).

You've got to know that when you feel overwhelmed, that's the time you should pour out your soul unto the Lord. You've got to be careful in the midst of being overwhelmed that you don't start doing the wrong thing, like pouring out your anger on other people or throwing up your hands and moving yourself out of the will of God.

#6—Old Sin Resurrects Itself

The sixth sign is when old iniquities begin to resurface again. Things that you hadn't battled with in a long time start sliding back into your behavior. Things that you were so glad that God loosed you from are now trying to inch their way back into your life. It's not so much the fact that they are there that bothers you. It's the fact that they are enticing you that bothers you. This disquiets you because there is a pull on you. And if it's pulling on you, then that means something is happening in your life that is weakening your spirit man. That's the only way old iniquities sneak back to the surface.

What we face once, we will face again.

Matthew 12:43–45 teaches that when an unclean spirit is gone out of a person, it walks through dry places seeking rest and finds none. Then it says, "I will return to the same house that I came out of." If it finds that house empty and clean and swept, it says, "I will go back and grab seven other spirits more evil than myself, and we will go back in." As a result, the end of that man is worse than it was at the beginning. We understand from this teaching that what we face once, we will face again. So we have to do more than just allow sins to go. We have to have the consciousness and the understanding that whatever God delivered us from, we will need to remain delivered from.

#7 — *Pulling Away from Godly Relationships*

Please take heed to this one. Remember it, because it is one of the fastest things to alert me, as a pastor, that someone is under attack. The devil doesn't want to hang around godly people. They make him sick. So when he's trying to set up residence in individuals, he'll quickly move to separate them from any holy, discerning, loving, praying people. People who have darkness attaching to them have to sequester themselves from people who carry around too much light.

When people begin to pull away from godly relationships, it is a dangerous sign. It should be to you, and it certainly should be to those around you. When people are filled with the things of God, they love to be with the saints of God. But when a person comes under attack, he goes into hiding.

> *When people are filled with the things of God, they love to be with the saints of God. But when a person is under attack, he goes into hiding.*

You have to be careful because the devil will make you think that your enemies are your friends and your friends are your enemies. Sometimes your friends are not always the ones who are agreeing with you. Sometimes your friends are the ones who will look you in your face and say, "You can do better than what you're doing right now, and I'm not going to agree with you, because you're wrong." Sometimes your enemies are not those who are disagreeing with you. Sometimes your enemies are those agreeing with you. You have to discern and know the difference.

You have to be careful when you begin to pull away from godly relationships. When you start getting to the point where you're justifying why you don't have any saved friends, and the only people you feel comfortable around are sinners, something is wrong. Naturally, if you don't have some friends who aren't saved, you wouldn't be much good to the kingdom. You'd be fishing in a fishbowl. But when your comfort zone becomes the company of sinners and your discomfort zone is among the saints, something is wrong.

It's amazing some of the hyper-spiritual comments people make when they are excusing their withdrawal. "Well, I'm tired of phony Christians. I just want be around some real people." You're trying to claim pure motives, but the truth is that you're running with people who don't challenge you and who won't hold you accountable to anything. Don't pull away from godly relationships. It's a bad sign.

#8 — Discouragement

Have you ever felt like giving up? Have you ever become overly discouraged? There's a distinction between this sign and the fifth sign of feeling overwhelmed. The difference is that when you feel like giving up, you start looking for a reason to give up. For example, so many times, before people divorce, they've already built their case so that they sound justified for what they're doing. Once you start looking for a reason, you find one.

When you start looking for a reason to give up on God, you'll find one. I have learned that it's impossible to keep someone planted whose feet tend to run. When you get it in your mind that you want to give up on God, quit going to church, or whatever, and you start looking for a reason, I'm telling you now that you will find that reason. Why? Because the devil will accommodate every desire you have to separate yourself from the body of Christ. He knows that if he can separate you, he has you. So he plants seeds of resentment, envy, persecution, and bitterness in you. Then he'll water them with a few lies like "Things will never change," and "Why do you bother? No one appreciates you." After that, all he has to do is sit back and wait for you to start looking for reasons to give up.

Christianity is for regular people. Jesus died so we could be the human beings we were created to be.

#9 — *You Have to Manufacture Excitement*

I believe that everybody needs hobbies, recreation, outlets, and things to do. It's okay to have fun; everything doesn't have to be serious. I personally know some people who don't know how to do anything but pray. Unfortunately, those people will never lead anybody to Christ. They have trouble relating to believers, let alone the unchurched. Christianity is for regular people. Jesus didn't die on the cross so we could be God; He died so we could be the human beings we were created to be. As I like to say, "Be light, but for goodness' sake, *lighten up!*"

I have found that when people come under spiritual attack, they've got to be careful about what energizes and fuels them. Let me say it this way. When you are in the life-flow of God, there is *energeo*. (That's a Greek word from which we get our English word *energy*.) That is, you are plugged into the life-giving energy of the Holy Spirit. When you're in that flow, there is an energy and a life force that you gain from praise and worship, from hearing the Word of God, from prayer and intercession, and from being with the saints of God.

When you disconnect from the life force of God, such as when you're under attack, you become numb. You're unable to be touched by the flow of God. Therefore, in an attempt to feel like you're alive, you will try to over-stimulate yourself some other way because you have no internal stimulation going. You have to see a scary movie so that you can remember what it's like to feel something. You have to read a love story so that you can remember what it feels like to feel something. People under attack in this way are always going from one thing to the next because they need something to give them a false feeling of being alive. They are looking for a feeling similar to the one they used to get from being a part of the flow of God.

People under attack look to other sources to provide the feelings they used to get from God.

These people are always on the run, always on the move, and never sitting still. They've got basketball on Monday night, bowling on Tuesday night, a date at the pool hall on Wednesday night, three movies and dinner out on Friday night, and on Saturday they have to buy something new to wear so they feel better. They just keep running, and they never sit down because if they ever get still and quiet, the Spirit of God begins to settle them.

Yes, you ought to have some time for fun. You ought to have some time to go to amusement parks, to take your family to a sporting event, or to go see a movie with your spouse. I hope it makes you fall in love with each other all over again. But when you do something to try to provoke a feeling that you no longer have on your own, it's a sign that you are under attack.

#10 — Looking Back

This last sign also is a dangerous one. You know you're a victim of this attack when you start looking back and longing for your former lifestyle. You start looking back on the way you used to live before God saved you, and you actually think that it was good. "I used to have some friends before I got saved. I used to have fun." You forget that it *God can make us battle-ready at a moment's notice.* was that lifestyle and those so-called friends that brought you weeping to the altar, saying, "God, I'll do anything, if You save my soul." You forgot the demons that you got delivered from. You forgot the bondages you were rescued from. So now you start looking back and wishing for the bad ol' days that seem like good ol' days in the midst of spiritual attack.

No doubt there are other signs of spiritual attack. There aren't enough pages in this book to deal with all the ways Satan tries to attack us. God, however, can make us battle-ready at a moment's notice. You see, there is no battle we face that we will have to fight alone, unless we choose to. Even then, God will work things out for our good. Still, I want to give you four things that will help you when you encounter a spiritual attack.

- **Do not forsake the place of prayer, which is God's connection to you.**

- **Do not forsake the place of power, which is God's house.**

- **Do not forsake the power of partnership, which is God's ministry to you through others.**

- **Do not forsake pastoral protection, which is God's covering for you.**

"Put on the whole armor of God, that you may be able to stand against the wiles of the devil" (Eph. 6:11). Make no mistake. You've got an enemy, and sooner or later you will have an encounter with him. Everybody will have to live through some attacks. But, if you protect yourself with God, then through Him you'll find out that standing through battles, adversities, and attacks meant to destroy you is just another way for God to lead you to a shout. Yes, there are cunning devices, chosen chariots, and weapons formed against your weaknesses, but guess what? No device of the enemy can bring you to ruin.

There is no battle that you face that you will have to fight alone—unless you choose to.

Nobody knows like you do how close you came to the edge. Nobody knows the weapons that were formed against you. Nobody knows how much you struggle, press, and push through when you don't feel like it. But hold on. All that weeping means that some joy is due you.

Never forget that when the attack heats up, your break-through can't be far away.

8
A Time for Peace

8
A Time for Peace

---◆◦◆◦◆---

*For peace is not mere absence of war, but it is a virtue that springs
from force of character.*
—Benedictus De Spinoza

*You will keep him in perfect peace, whose mind is
stayed on You, because he trusts in You.*
—Isaiah 26:3

There is a truth that I believe the Holy Spirit has been
working on giving to the body of Christ for a long
time. We can find it in chapter 5 of Matthew. This
is Jesus' Sermon on the Mount, and in it are things that
are often read but not often understood or appreciated.
Let's take a look at a powerful nugget in the center of His
"Beatitudes," which is Jesus' discourse on the blessedness
of man.

> *Blessed are the peacemakers, for they shall be called sons of God.*   (Matt. 5:9)

Ecclesiastes 3:1 says there is a time and a season to every purpose under heaven. Following that opening verse is a listing of every possible purpose for which there could be a season or an appointed time. In the previous chapter we talked about spiritual warfare. But Solomon says in Ecclesiastes that there is also a season or a time for peace. Then, as we read in Matthew 5:9, Jesus went on to say that not only is there a time for peace, but also the people who go out of their way to make peace shall be called the sons (and daughters) of God. So in this chapter I want to focus on peace.

Have you ever noticed that when Jesus takes it upon Himself to teach us something, it almost always stretches us beyond what we're comfortable with? That it almost always calls us to do things, reach for things, or embrace things that are contrary to our human

Jesus doesn't bother to teach us things that come easy to us. He stretches us beyond what we're comfortable with.

nature? He doesn't bother too much with the things that come easy to us. Most of Jesus' teachings don't center on what we're already good at. He almost always focuses on the areas that we don't think about, or don't want to.

"Love your enemies." That's in the same passage of Matthew 5. You know that's a stretch for most of us. *"Do good to those who hate you."* I don't know about you, but I was not born with that in me. It's as though Jesus deliberately shines the spotlight on stuff He knows we struggle with.

When I first began to look at this issue of being a peacemaker, I thought, *Here we go again.* There is a time for peace, and when we choose peace in those seasons, we are blessed by God as His children. But, making peace—like loving your enemies and praying for those who use you—is contrary to convenient, comfortable, cosmetic, cuddly Christianity. It's hard. Then it hit me. I began to see that we have to fight for all the things of God, not just some of them. We know that there's a time for war. That's easy to figure out. But the Lord showed me that His people have to be as armed and as ready to obtain peace.

Have you ever come to a place in your life where you're just tired of wrestling and struggling? It's a necessary place. You have to come to the point where you get tired of fighting with people and things that are going on around you and in you.

When you get to the place where peace is yours no matter what, you are blessed.

You come to the place where you've got to find some peace. And when you can't find any peace, you determine to learn how to make some. When you get there—when you get to that place where peace is yours no matter what—Jesus said you are blessed.

Blessed are the manufacturers of peace. Blessed are the people who can make peace where there is none, for they shall be called the children of God. Children of God make peace. They make it and keep it in themselves. They toss a little bit of it in the midst of contention and strife between others. They look for it, value it, and refuse to trade it for anything.

When you step back and, with an objective eye, analyze religious people and the church as a whole, you see a lot of things done in the name of God that are really just the by-products of somebody's anger and frustration. There's no peace in it. For example, a lot of preaching is done with anger. Many people who think they're praying strong are just praying loud because they're mad. Religious people are angry people. I'm not talking about saved people; I'm talking about "religious" people. They're mad because when you're religious, you always come up short and can't be happy. Religion locks up, isolates, and frustrates people. If you are religious, everybody else is wrong and you're right, because you have convinced yourself that no one is holier than you are.

Of course, angry people aren't the only people without peace. People without faith are usually without peace as well. There are people in sin without peace. People who are bitter have no peace. People with too much "good work" and not enough "God work" to do are never at peace either. You've seen "Sister Martha" at church, running around like a holy headless chicken, jack of all ministries and master of none. She's frustrated and mad because nobody appreciates her. And when someone suggests that she might be too busy, she rebukes that person for trying to steal, kill, and destroy her ministry.

If God calls you to do something, His peace will go with you.

We do need workers in the church, but if God called you to do something, His peace always goes with you.

God wants to anoint His people with peace. He wants every part of you to be covered with peace—from head to sole and sole to *soul*. Yes, there is a time to do battle. We're good at fighting for what we want. We're skilled at brandishing our swords in the face of all who stand against us. However, part of becoming all that God has called you to involves learning how to be at peace, be in peace, and pursue peace. After all, Jesus is the Prince of Peace. And if His Spirit is in us, then we have to make finding peace a priority in our Christian walk.

This was a hard one for me. I'm a fighter by nature. If I believe in something, I usually plant my feet in the ground and fight, "come hell or high water." If an enemy's trying to take over my boat, I'll sink it with him and me in it before I'll let him have it. Whatever the devil has tried to rob, I'll take back. Jesus and I, we will fight. But the Lord whispered something in my ear one day that shook me up. He said, "You have been faithful to follow Me into battle. Will you be faithful now to follow Me into peace?" I ask you that same question. Are you willing to follow God into peace? Blessed are those who can manufacture peace, for they shall be called the children of God.

We have to make finding peace a priority in our Christian walk.

A Picture of Peace

The average person understands peace to be some state of being that is without noise. That couldn't be further from the truth. Actually, that defines *quiet*, not peace. Sometimes quiet can mean that you're just avoiding something. Avoidance is not peace. Quiet can mean that I'm not speaking to you or you're not speaking to me because we're angry. Resentment and unforgiveness can be really quiet, but they are not peaceful. Just ask any married person. It's called the "silent treatment," not the peaceful treatment. So there are a few things that peace is not. Let's got through those first.

First of all, peace is not the absence of trouble. Remember the story of the disciples in the boat with the storm raging all around them? In the midst of all that chaos, Jesus stood up and said, "Peace, be still" (Mark 4:39). That tells me it's possible to have peace in the midst of the storm.

Now this next one may shock you, but peace is not the absence of enemies either. This is important. Peace does not mean that you don't have any enemies. Peace means that no enemies have you as an enemy. Do you understand that? *You* are not an enemy.

Peace means that you are the enemy of no man. Psalm 23 says that God can prepare a table for you in the presence of your enemies. That means there will be times when you are surrounded by enemies and feasting with Jehovah Shalom. Jesus also said to love your enemies (Matt 5:44). That means there will be people against you. Peace does not mean that folks aren't against you or that some folks don't oppose you. Peace means that *you* are the enemy of no man. You might be an enemy against me, but I am not against you. You might be seeking to do me harm, but I will not seek to do you harm. That's the stretching part for me!

I know this one shakes us up a bit because many of us get more excited about going into battle. When we find out that opposers and accusers are arrayed against us, we shout and clap and get ready to go to battle. We forget that the Bible says we cannot repay evil for evil. Jesus said that we are to seek to bless those who are trying to do evil to us (Matt. 5:44). That is how we are known as the children of God in the midst of the world. To be at peace doesn't mean that no one is against us.

At the same time, this doesn't mean that you put your enemies in a position where they can harm you. Don't allow somebody into your inner circle if you know that he is plotting your destruction. But don't spend time plotting his either. Spend your time asking God how you can bless that person.

Believe me, this is easier to say than to live out. We are all human. Nevertheless, this is what Jesus said.

When the Lord whispered to me to follow Him into peace, He showed me that the next phase of my ministry would be different from the previous one. I was known as the young warrior who conquered kingdoms of this world. But He said that if I would follow Him, He would make me a peacemaker. He told me that people would take me into a new season wherein I would be known as a peacemaker, as a bearer of peace. Now, that didn't mean I was special or that my church was special. Becoming peacemakers is God's promise to us all. You see, when Matthew 5:9 says that the peacemakers will become the *"sons of God,"* *"sons"* refers to mature sons (and daughters). So in other words, God was telling me that if I would follow Him, He would usher me into a more mature walk with Him. Young people fight. Young lions roar and do battle. Those who have some time and experience behind them, though, stop looking for fights and start looking for peace.

Young David had slain both a lion and a bear before he took on Goliath. The Bible says that when he fought Goliath, he ran up to the Philistine to shoot him with that slingshot. David was eager and ready for a fight. But, as he matures, we see him less anxious to do battle and more concerned with peace—peace with Saul, peace for Israel, peace in his household. When David was young, he was looking for God to get in there and fight with him. By the time he became king, he was a man pursuing peace between Judah and Israel, and battle was simply a means to achieve rest from their enemies.

As we walk with God, He matures us and makes us wise. We grow in maturity and are most like God when we are at peace. You see, war takes. We fight to take authority over the enemy. Peace, on the other hand, gives. It is a gift from Jesus, and it is the gift *of* Jesus. That's why Jesus said, *"My peace I give to you"* (John 14:27).

We grow in maturity and are most like God when we are at peace.

I am embracing God's peace in my life. It amazes me now, the people who get upset with me because I refuse to get upset with those whom they're upset with. They want me to be mad at the people they're mad at. They think I'm supposed to have a problem with so-and-so because they have a problem with him. And they get mad when I don't. The point is, peace is something that you have to carry around in your spirit.

Please understand that peace must be untainted, unconditional, unselfish, and unrestricted when we offer it to others. Otherwise, it becomes the offering of Judas—a betrayal with a kiss. We can't pretend to be at peace with someone or lie about our desire for it. We can't offer it with strings attached, or offer it today and take it back tomorrow. So much of what passes for peace between believers today is quiet, cool, detached piety. That's false peace, and it separates people. True peace that comes from Jesus brings people together.

The kind of peace that we're supposed to have is not just peace that comes. It is peace that abides. When Jesus offered to give His disciples His peace in John 14:27, He implied that it would be a peace that would be left with them. You see, He gave them peace in their hearts.

We have that same peace, and by it we are known as the children of God because it is the peace that comes from Him. The world can't give you this peace. The world can't give you the ability to be at peace with all men, to be at peace in the midst of a storm, to have peace even with conflict around you on every side, or to impart peace in a person's home or amongst his family.

Peace that comes from Jesus brings people together.

Peace is God's signature upon our hearts. It is His mark upon our foreheads. It says we belong to God. We've all seen children who look just like their parents. Folk say, "That child looks like his daddy spit him out." That's how it is with us. When we walk around looking like peace, talking like peace, walking like peace, and handing out peace like we've got it on sale, we look like the "spittin' image" of our Daddy. Jesus told the scribes and Pharisees that their hypocritical behavior made them look like their father the devil. In Matthew 5 He told us that being a peacemaker makes us look like our Father.

The Atmosphere of Peace

True peace operates effectively in our lives only when we understand and respect God's timing, God's sovereignty, and God's omniscience. Peace comes when I can say, believe, and accept that there are some things not for this season, or were for last season. It comes when I'm able to accept and believe that God can do whatever He wants to, when He wants to, and in whatever manner that suits Him. Lastly, true peace comes when I can believe, accept, and say that whatever happens, God is always right. If everything in me disagrees with His methods, then the only conclusion I can draw is that I must be wrong, since God is always right. For better or worse, God is right. In sickness or health, happiness or sorrow, God is always right. In the company of people or walking alone, God is right. On the mountaintop or in the valley, God is right. Get into the habit of saying that whenever you're tempted to complain or fall into discontentment.

You cannot be at peace when you are trying to change things that you cannot change. Neither can you be at peace when you are trying to change people whom you cannot change. Peace comes when you understand that there is a purpose and a season for everything. There are some things you can change right now. And there are other things that right now you can't change, but later on will be able to change. So be at peace and deal with what you can deal with now. Thus peace comes when we understand the principles of God's timing, sovereignty, and omniscience.

Peace also comes when we understand the words of Jesus when He told Peter, *"All who take the sword will perish by the sword"* (Matt. 26:52). If drama, strife, and contention are all we know, then we will never become peace manufacturers. If we don't become makers and carriers of peace, the children of God, then we will be like the apostle Peter—zealous without wisdom.

Now, you need to understand something about Peter. God knew He was hotheaded. That's partly why He chose him to be a disciple. Let me digress for a moment. God called you out of the world, yes, but He also called you *up*. He knew your personality; in fact, He designed it. He expects you to be holy, but He doesn't expect you to forsake your whole personality. Peter was a man who would stand up in the midst of a crowd and take everybody on. It was in his nature to do that. Jesus knew that when He saw him on that fishing boat and decided, "The kingdom could use a guy like that. He's going to be the first one out of the boat, the first one with his mouth open, the first one to jump into a fight, and the first one to defend Me. He's in it to win it. We could use a guy like Peter." He just needed a little work and a little training in the art of "peaceful protest."

> *God called you out of the world, but He doesn't expect you to forsake your personality.*

Sometimes Peter didn't know how to manufacture peace. His spirit was willing—and God can always use a willing spirit—but his flesh was weak. He was always more ready to fight or cuss somebody out. When the soldiers came to arrest Jesus, Peter was in rare form. He jumped up, grabbed a sword, and cut off a man's ear. Remember, this was one of the men coming to take Jesus to be crucified. And Jesus had just told Peter and the disciples that He had to die and that His death would save the world. Yet, here's Peter trying to save His life. It's sort of funny when you think about it: Peter was trying to save the Savior!

If Peter had been paying attention and praying when Jesus had told him to, he would have realized that he was about to abort the whole purpose for which Jesus was born. Instead, Jesus had to reach down, take that ear, and put it back on that man's head. Blessed are the peacemakers.

Here's the problem with living by the sword. In order to function or move through life, you always have to have an enemy, and you always have to fight *War takes you into* him. Sooner or later, you will run into *the valley, but peace* an enemy who's going to take you out. *will take you to the* Paul, on the other hand, said to the *high places.* Romans, *"How beautiful are the feet of those who preach the gospel of peace, who bring glad tidings of good things"* (Rom. 10:15). Paul was in fact paraphrasing the prophet Isaiah, who declared, *"How beautiful upon the mountains are the feet of him who brings good news, who proclaims peace"* (Isa. 52:7). War takes you into the valley, but peace will take you to the high places. Now, there's nothing wrong with the valley; there's nothing bad, per se, about the low places that God takes us to. We are purged and tried in the valley. The valley has great value. Ultimately, however, He wants us to meet Him in the high places. We are lights set on a hill; we are people who "go up" to Zion. Our journey to God is one of ascent. As the song says, we're "goin' up yonder" to be with the Lord.

Now it shall come to pass in the latter days that the mountain of the LORD's house shall be established on the top of the mountains, and shall be exalted above the hills; and all nations shall flow to it. Many people shall come and say, "Come, and let us go up to the mountain of the LORD, to the house of the God of Jacob; He will teach us His ways, and we will walk in His paths." For out of Zion shall go forth the law, and the word of the LORD from Jerusalem. He shall judge between the nations, and rebuke many people; they shall beat their swords into plowshares, and their spears into pruning hooks; nation shall not lift up sword against nation, neither shall they learn war anymore. (Isa. 2:2–4)

Here Isaiah paints a landscape of true peace. This passage is a prophecy of the future reign of Jesus Christ, which will bring about an end to all war on the earth. This is a prophecy of the coming Prince of Peace. *"You've been faithful to follow Me into battle. Will you now be faithful to follow Me into peace?"*

Those words rose up in my spirit again as I studied this passage. Then the Lord began to tell me that He would show us power in the midst of peace that we have not known, even in the midst of warfare. I began to meditate on that as I read these Scriptures over and over again. Whenever I tried to stop, the Holy Spirit would say, "Read it again." So I'd read it again. And again. And again. And then I got it.

Peace prepares you for harvest.

God said through His prophet Isaiah that there was coming a day when He would speak peace. And when He does, His people will take their swords and their spears and beat them into plowshares and pruning hooks. Here's the key: Peace prepares you for harvest. Plowshares and pruning hooks are instruments of harvest.

God said that we will go from fighting to reaping the harvest that we've been fighting for. We're going to take those swords, beat them down, and plow up some land with it. We're going to take those spears and use them for pruning hooks. God is getting ready to take His people from doing battle to gathering up blessings.

After all, what are we fighting for anyway? Some people have fought for so long that they think the fight is the objective. It's not. The reason that we war is to produce an atmosphere by which the harvest can be taken in. So God has us take our instruments of war and use them as instruments of harvest. War and peace are not extremes or opposites of one another; rather, they are the two parts of a metamorphosis or change. War is a caterpillar. Peace is the stunning butterfly that comes from it.

War is a caterpillar. Peace is the stunning butterfly that comes from it.

The next thing you need to know about the atmosphere of peace is that peace comes when you recognize God's purpose behind everything. When Judas and the soldiers of the high priest came to take Jesus away, Jesus was at peace because He knew that they were unwittingly serving God's purpose. He knew He came to die. These men were simply helping God's kingdom to come and making sure His will was done on earth as it is in heaven.

Don't boast that all things work together for your good when you can only take the good stuff. Even the things the enemy sends to harm you—those things and people who come against you—are included in "all things." These things will come. Otherwise, how can Jesus say that you are blessed when people persecute you and talk about you, if nobody ever does it?

Some of us fall into a victimization mentality. We walk around feeling like everybody's against us, nobody loves us, and somebody's talking about us. Then, because we're hurt and angry, we think it's okay to retaliate, and call it spiritual warfare. Blessed are the peacemakers, the ones who understand that God is in control, for they shall be called the children of God.

Peace is yours when you believe that there are more for you than against you. You can never be at peace in your life when you think that you're outnumbered. *"If God is for us, who can be against us?"* (Rom. 8:31).

Peacemakers understand that God is in control.

There's a powerful picture of this kind of peace in 2 Kings 6:8-23. The older prophet Elisha lives at peace, with peace, and in peace. He's calm. "No problem" and "no sweat" are phrases that apply. His nervous servant, on the other hand, is running around outside, freaking out. That's the picture of strife, not peace. Of course, can you really blame him? While they were asleep, the Syrian army surrounded the city to capture the prophet. The king sent a whole army after one man. What makes you think the enemy won't set up a host against you when you start doing the Lord's work?

So here's the entire army surrounding their city, and the little servant with Elisha is scared. Many people want a king-sized anointing, but they don't have enough peace to handle the king-sized fights that come with it. You see, the combat isn't hand-to-hand when you get to Elisha's level. It's spirit to spirit.

This young man woke up and saw all the soldiers outside, and he told Elisha, "Do you know what's going on out here? It's time to fight! There's a battle waiting for us out there."

"What do you mean?" Elisha said.

"Look, look!" the servant pointed. "Look at the problem! We're surrounded. Get ready to fight! Get a sword! Borrow one if you have to! You're the prophet; do something!"

So he answered, "Do not fear, for those who are with us are more than those who are with them." And Elisha prayed, and said, "Lord, I pray, open his eyes that he may see." (2 Kings 6:16–17)

Picture this scenario. This boy sees horses, soldiers, swords, scowls, and frowns all directed at him and this man of God he was crazy enough to get hooked up with. He's thinking, *Elisha, you have lost your mind. Open my eyes?! I can see. There's two of us, and one, two, three, four—a zillion of them! Do the math. I'm not even a prophet, and I can tell that we're toast.*

But Elisha has peace. And he's praying that God would give his servant some. "Lord, let his eyes be opened."

Then the Lord opened the eyes of the young man, and he saw. And behold, the mountain was full of horses and chariots of fire all around Elisha. (v. 17)

You can be at peace only when you know there are more for you than there are against you. You cannot be at peace when you focus on the people who don't like you, the person who is upset with you, or the whole gang talking behind your back. You're seeing with the wrong eyes then. You can't win that way. Don't lose your peace just because other people aren't at peace with you. The fact is, you can't be a Christian and not have enemies. Jesus had plenty, and He's our example. So get over it and get on with kingdom business.

True peace is yours when you make up your mind that it is the most valuable tool you have for working out your salvation. It's yours when you decide that there is nothing worth trading it for. Abraham understood that. He was a man blessed by God and who heard from God. One day God told him, "I'm going to bless you, and My blessing includes dealing with your enemies." God promised to bless the people who blessed Abraham, but He also promised to curse the people who cursed him. God personally dealt with anybody who thought he was big or bad enough to rise up against Abraham. Some of us today would have let that go to our heads. But here's what happened in Abraham's case.

You can't be a Christian and not have enemies.

Abraham was traveling with his nephew Lot. Lot, unfortunately, was selfish, carnal, and ungrateful. He was a peace robber rather than a peacemaker. You've seen the type. Such people don't want to do too much work, but they're the first ones to show up when your hard work pays off. They'll cheat you behind your back and then get in your face and talk about the importance of "family." That was Lot. As the son of Abraham's brother, he knew he could count on Uncle Abraham to cut him some slack on a regular basis.

Abraham, however, wasn't stupid. He knew that Lot was trifling and irresponsible. But Lot was family, so Abraham put up with a lot from him. He even saved his life once.

Lot was someone who really should have understood his indebtedness to Abraham. He should have realized and appreciated the fact that he was being blessed because of Abraham. He was blessed by association, but he didn't acknowledge it or respect it. If we were in Abraham's shoes, I'm sure we would have found it hard to keep our peace. But then Lot made the situation worse when his herdsmen started contending with Abraham's herdsmen. It was bad enough that Abraham had been helping him all this time and Lot said nothing about it. Now Lot was rising up against Abraham. But Abraham handled it like a child of God.

Genesis 13 tells the story. Abraham went to Lot and said, *"Let there be no strife between you and me."* But he didn't stop there. Abraham continued, "Look, instead of telling you what I want, why don't you tell me what you want? Tell me where you want to go and which piece of property you want to pitch your tent on. I'll let you go and be at peace. In fact, if you want, I'll go the other way so we can be at peace." Abraham would rather let go of stuff than to lose his peace. He'd rather switch than fight. Remember, God had already promised Abraham regarding his enemies, so it's not as though Lot had a chance of winning any battle against him.

When you understand how valuable peace is, you won't surrender it to anybody for any reason. It needs to become more important to you than anything you could gain by fighting. If Christians could ever get as excited over the power of peace as we do over strife and contention, we'd really be doing something.

I don't want to suggest by any means that you won't have any conflict in peace. As was said before, peace is not just the absence of noise or the absence of opposition. You are supposed to endure some things. Hebrews 12 says that the Lord chastens the ones He loves. It goes on to point out that if we're not feeling a little heat from time to time, God may be dealing with us as He would kids who didn't belong to Him. (See Hebrews 12:5–8.) If you're not going through something, then you might need to question your status as a child of God.

When you understand how valuable peace is, you won't surrender it to anybody for any reason.

The Point of Peace

Peace is the way of power. Let me repeat that: The way of peace is the way of power. Some people believe that in order to be at peace you have to be weak, and that somehow means everybody just runs all over you. On the contrary, it takes more strength to be at peace than it does to wield a weapon.

When the Roman soldiers took Jesus away to be crucified, the Bible says, *"He was led as a sheep to the slaughter,* and as a lamb before its shearer is silent, so He opened not his mouth" (Acts 8:32). If Jesus had wanted to, He could have summoned legions of angels to come and to defend Him and get Him off that cross. But as a lamb before its shearer, He would not open His mouth. That took more strength. Peace is restraint; that is, it is power under control. From this perspective, peace is not just for our benefit, but also for the benefit of others.

The power of peace, for example, is the pathway of acceptance. When you walk in peace, other people come into your life. Ask yourself from time to time if people are moving toward you or away from you. Is your circle of friends and influence getting bigger, or is it getting smaller? People will avoid you if they feel like you don't or won't accept them.

It takes more strength to be at peace than it does to wield a weapon.

We struggle with this aspect of peace. We like to say, "Well, I don't want to accept everything those people do. I can't accept them because of their lifestyles." Nobody's talking about what they do. Why was it that everyone felt comfortable coming to Jesus? Sinners, wine bibbers, Samaritans, the woman at the well, the woman taken in the act of adultery—they all gathered to Jesus. He was perfect in His holiness, yet He was the friend of Mary Magdalene who had had seven devils. Now, Jesus never once condoned sin; He never ignored it or excused it. But to all He said, "Come." In the same way, when we carry peace, the people who need help can move toward us. I believe a lot of churches are empty today because there is no peace there. People avoid them because they do not feel like they are accepted.

The power of peace is not just the pathway of acceptance, but it also is the key that unlocks the heart. Why is that important? People carry secrets in their hearts. People put on facades and good fronts. They stand there pretending that they've got it all together when that's the last thing they've got. So many of our young people in the world today play bad and play hard. Why? It keeps people away from them. They're hurting and scared, and they don't trust anybody to lead them out of their dark places. But when you carry peace, that peace becomes the key that unlocks their hearts, because a peaceful spirit is a discerning one.

Finally, the power of peace is the power of love. It is the power that works through love. It gives you the power to love, actually. Peace is the power of love in operation. If you have love in you and working around you, then you can be at peace with people.

Jesus, the Prince of Peace, loves people. In fact, He knows more about us than we know about ourselves, so even if we hate ourselves, He refuses to do anything but love us. The peace that He carries and leaves with us is the product of the love that He has toward us.

The power of peace is the power to love people, forgive them, bear their burdens, protect them, suffer long with them, and have compassion for them. Do you love someone enough to suffer his indignities even if he proves to be less than what you imagined a friend to be? Peace makes staying in love possible. The devil's power is in the storms he creates in and between people. The Prince of Peace rebukes storms and declares them inactive, ineffective, and insignificant.

Blessed are the peacemakers, for they shall see miracles; heal wounds; expose the wiles of the enemy; move mountains; still storms; inspire, profess, and protect love; and be called the children of God.

9
Uncommon Love

9
Uncommon Love

◆◂◆◂◆

The issue is not what God is like. The issue is what kind of people we become when we attach ourselves to God.
—Rabbi Harold S. Kushner

Beloved, now are we the children of God; and it has not yet been revealed what we shall be, but we know that when He is revealed, we shall be like Him, for we shall see Him as He is.
—1 John 3:2

This may seem like an odd topic to end a book on, but it will make sense to you soon.

We've been studying, examining, and considering different aspects of the Christian life as it relates to God's desire that we live beyond our expectations and into His. The goal of every believer is, in the words of the apostle Paul, to *"mortify the deeds of the body"* and *"put on Christ"*

(Rom. 8:13 KJV; Gal. 3:27). That is, we must allow Him to be resurrected daily in our every word and deed.

> *I have been crucified with Christ; it is no longer I who live, but Christ lives in me; and the life which I now live in the flesh I live by faith in the Son of God, who loved me and gave Himself for me.* (Gal. 2:20)

We know now that the only way to live out our destiny as the people of God is to allow God to "wake up" or enlighten our hearts to His will and His ways. God speaks to our hearts through His Word. He repairs our broken hearts patiently and tenderly, miraculously bringing forth a harvest of joy equal to the weeping we sowed in our night seasons. He stabilizes and solidifies our hearts through the knowledge of our identity in Him.

We know that the Word of God framed the world and everything in it, and that as sons and daughters of God our mouths frame much of our reality and shape the lives of those around us. We can choose—through ignorance, bitterness, or brokenness—to fashion a frame that supports the lies of the devil. Or we can choose the truth and allow our mouths to confirm and affirm the victory that was ours before beginning began. Life and death are in the power of the tongue, and miracles come to those who choose life.

We learned that no Christian walk is undertaken free of conflict. Satan is hungry to destroy God's highest creation, and his appetite hasn't changed since he slithered into Eden. He still wants to devour our communion with God, and he'll take advantage of every opportunity to attack us. He knows our weaknesses and our vulnerabilities and forms his weapons against us accordingly. But the very thing he's after is what will protect us in the day of trouble, and that is our communion with God. If God be for us, who can be against us?

Finally, we understand that while spiritual warfare is a necessary part of uncommon living, the gift of peace is even more essential. There is a time for war, but the time for peace has a power all its own. We see God, hear Him, and understand Him better in an atmosphere of peace. True peace is a gift from God, and it is also the gift *of* God, since by it we are known as His children. Blessed is the man or woman who can manufacture peace in strife, conflict, and amidst persecution. Peace in us, through us, and on us is the greatest evidence of our maturity in Christ, for we find in it love, which is the glory of God.

That brings us to this point. And here I want to take you to 1 Corinthians 13, sometimes called "the love chapter" of the Bible. Most of us have read this passage, many of us several times. In it Paul talked to the people at the church in Corinth about how they should be acting, reacting, and interacting as believers.

Though I speak with the tongues of men and of angels, but have not love, I have become sounding brass or a clanging cymbal. And though I have the gift of prophecy, and understand all mysteries and all knowledge, and though I have all faith, so that I could remove mountains, but have not love, I am nothing. And though I bestow all my goods to feed the poor, and though I give my body to be burned, but have not love, it profits me nothing. Love suffers long and is kind; love does not envy; love does not parade itself, is not puffed up; does not behave rudely, does not seek its own, is not provoked, thinks no evil; does not rejoice in iniquity, but rejoices in the truth; bears all things, believes all things, hopes all things, endures all things. Love never fails. But whether there are prophecies, they will fail; whether there are tongues, they will cease; whether there is knowledge, it will vanish away. For we know in part and we prophesy in part. But when that which is perfect has come, then that which is in part will be done away. When I was a child, I spoke as a child, I understood as a child, I thought as a child; but when I became a man, I put away childish things. For now we see in a mirror, dimly, but then face to face. Now I know in part, but then I shall know just as I also am known. And now abide faith, hope, love, these three; but the greatest of these is love.

This is a powerful portion of Scripture. I think it would do us all good to read it more often and really start thinking about the kind of life that love lives. For now, though, I want to look at this passage from an angle that you may not have considered before.

Why the Corinthians?

The first and second books of Corinthians are letters written by the apostle Paul to believers in Corinth. Corinth was an interesting place at that time. It was a port city, a common stop for ships traveling throughout the Mediterranean Sea. A very prosperous area, it was a center of activity and commerce. People from all over the world came through Corinth to do business or to rest while on their way to somewhere else. Not surprisingly, Corinth was, therefore, a culturally diverse city, filled with all kinds of different people with different customs, practices, and philosophies. It was a cosmopolitan city—and kind of wild. The very diversity that made Corinth interesting also made it less connected to and certainly less constrained by traditional ethics and decorum.

But the Gospel came to Corinth, initially and primarily through the apostle Paul. He began to preach there, and believers began to grab hold of the Truth with the unrestricted passion that seemed to characterize that city. The Corinthians had a heart for God, and they moved toward Him with zeal. They just went for it with everything they had. It didn't take long for most everybody who knew about Corinth to hear something about the Christian believers there.

Knowing this, it shouldn't surprise us that the "love chapter" is found in Paul's letter to the Corinthians. A discourse on love belongs in a communication to people with a passion for God, right? But a close look through the chapters that lead up to 1 Corinthians 13 reveals a very disturbing set of circumstances. We find out in those chapters that Paul was not actually writing to commend the Corinthian church. He wrote 1 Corinthians to correct them. They were caught up, tied up, and tangled up in a lot of sin, and the love chapter follows a long discussion exposing that sin and exhorting believers to remember the promises they made to God.

I want to end our discussion in this book with 1 Corinthians for two reasons. First, it's important to see that the life God has called us to is not defined by our ability to "have church." The Corinthian Christians thought that they were truly spiritual. They thought they were spiritual because no church could touch them when it came to the more visible indicators of spirituality. They could prophesy with the best of them. They had seen miracles and spoken in tongues. An abundance of spiritual gifts was operating among them.

The truth is, although they were spiritually gifted, they were not spiritual people. In fact, Paul called them carnal. Paul saw that they were putting too much emphasis on their spiritual gifts and forgetting the Spirit behind the gifts. They thought that as long as they understood how to behave like they were connected to God while they were in church, that they could leave there and live any kind of way the rest of the week and still be considered holy. So Paul wrote to them. He told them that their hearts had to get to a place where the love of Jesus Christ ruled and reigned, or all their religious behavior—the tongues, prophecy, giving, etc.— would be in vain. That's the second thing I want to look at in this passage. The life God wants us to live—that life where we are dead to self, intimate with Him, and propelled by His Holy Spirit—is a life of love.

The life God wants us to live is a life of love.

I know we would rather hear about cars, riches, spouses, and prosperity. A lot of books equate those things with abundant living. And certainly they do have something to do with it. But, ultimately, the life of the crucified saint—the one who knows the fellowship of Christ's suffering, is conformable unto His death, and strives to live in resurrection power—is one who embraces and embodies love.

When God really works on us, we go beyond acting like we're His to really being His. If what you learn in these pages doesn't extend to how you treat others, you have not reached uncommon living. Remember, the bride of Christ is not an individual; it is the corporate body of believers. Because the Spirit of God drives us, and God is love, then we are driven by love as well. So we can say all the right words, believe all the right things, identify ourselves with the Father, claim His Son as our Savior, and operate in the gifts of the Holy Spirit, but if we don't love one another, it won't count for anything.

A miraculous life is more than just a life that has witnessed miracles. It is one that God can use miraculously to transform others into His image. We are all different, but the one thing we have in common is the love of God dwelling in us. So I want to suggest to you that if your life's goal is to use your relationship with God to heal yourself, enrich yourself, empower yourself, or advance yourself, then you have fallen short of God's plans for you.

The abundant life, the eternal life, the prosperous life, is a life directed by, powered by, and perfected by love. And love always has an object. We're used to dealing with the Word of God on an individual level, but whenever God deals with love, He's dealing with us in our corporate understanding of Him.

Friend, if we are going to get our hearts right, then we cannot measure spirituality the way some people measure it. It is not determined by goose bumps or dreams and visions, by how much money someone gives, or by how beautiful people sound when they speak in tongues.

Somewhere in our hearts we must be rooted and grounded in the knowledge of Jesus Christ. It is that knowledge that produces some things in our lives. It produces the things that are listed in 1 Corinthians 13. Let me say it this way. It doesn't matter what gifts we can function in if we are still short-tempered, easily provoked, or lacking in compassion and patience.

We must be rooted and grounded in the knowledge of Jesus Christ.

How's your love life? It's time to take a check. We're going to take a look at 1 Corinthians and apply that cold, hard truth to ourselves. Let me warn you now. If you're just playing church, Paul's letter is going to hurt your feelings. If you get upset, don't blame me. Talk to Paul about it when you get to heaven. These are his words.

Let's begin in chapter 1.

Taking Stock of Our Lives

> *You come short in no gift, eagerly waiting for the revelation of our Lord Jesus Christ.* (1 Cor. 1:7)

Paul began by building up the Corinthians believers. He said that when it came to spiritual gifts, the Corinthians were not behind anybody. They could do it with the best of them. They could sing with the best of them. They could prophesy with the best of them. They knew the difference between a prophetic flow and an evangelistic flow. They understood all the spiritual things that were going on. He acknowledged all that, but then he turned the tables on them. He began to show them why they weren't quite as spiritual as they thought they were.

> *Now I plead with you, brethren, by the name of our Lord Jesus Christ, that you all speak the same thing, and that there be no divisions among you, but that you be perfectly joined together in the same mind and in the same judgment. For it has been declared to me concerning you, my brethren, by those of Chloe's household, that there are contentions among you.* (1 Cor. 1:10–11)

They were not spiritual because they were divided. As long as you are inciting or participating in divisions between your brothers and sisters in the church, Paul said there's a problem.

In one sense the apostle Paul was writing to a people that could prophesy to one another, but couldn't get along with each other. They were busy impressing one another, but there were divisions among them. Remember, we're going to end up at the love chapter. Paul's goal was to get the Corinthians to be a loving people—a people who walk in the Spirit of God, who is love. He wanted to show them what was wrong and how they needed to correct it. And the first problem he tackled was that they were divided.

When God calls people together, He gives them a vision for the house—one vision. If there's any more than one vision, the house becomes divided. "Di-vision" simply means two visions. It's amazing how people who think they are spiritual sometimes use their supposed spirituality to be in disagreement with the vision of the house. God gave a vision, then all of a sudden they say, "Well, I really think maybe we should do it this way or that way." They claim to be operating in gifts of discernment and wisdom when, in actuality, they're allowing themselves to be used by the enemy to divide the house. Paul addressed that issue when he told the Corinthians to learn to say the same thing. How can two walk together unless they agree? How can we say we're a church that walks with God if we don't agree with His vision for our house?

Why is it that some people can't get along with anybody? Why is it that some people, no matter how good the Spirit of God is moving or how great God is blessing, always have another opinion? If you stand up, they are going to sit down. If you sit down, they are going to stand up. If you say clap, they say wave. If you say wave, they say clap. If you say it's time to give, they want to pray. If you say it's time to pray, they want to give. There's always somebody who has something in him that is contrary to what God says everybody should be doing at that time.

How can we say we're a church that walks with God if we don't agree with His vision?

If we are going to be mature people, then we must have the capacity to be unified with those who are in the household of faith. This is important, because the more people God adds to His church, the more potential there is for them to be at odds with one another. The fact is, people simply have different personalities. But if those differences ever become bigger than the work that God has called us to do together, then we cannot consider ourselves to be spiritually mature. Maturity means having the ability to bear the infirmities of the weak. That means those who are more mature have greater tolerance, not less. Some people consider their spirituality to be greater because they can't tolerate anything. They can't tolerate other people's failures, weaknesses, or differences. That is not a sign of maturity; that is a sign of infancy. It's a sign of immaturity.

When you become mature, you have the ability to forbear one another. You already know that people are not perfect. So why should you be surprised when they act in a way that just confirms what you already know about them? Quit getting upset every time somebody acts like he still lives in flesh and blood. Get over thinking that people are flawless and fail-proof. Get over thinking that people who have gifts functioning in their lives are automatically mature. Get over thinking that everybody who has a title or a position is superhuman. Get over it, because there is only One who is perfect, and He was crucified. Now He's bringing us into perfection, but we are not there yet.

> *Quit getting upset every time somebody acts like he still lives in flesh and blood.*

Neither is a unified church a church full of clones. I think that a pastor or any leader who surrounds him or herself with a bunch of "yes people" is foolish. At the same time, it is essential for any organized entity—secular included—to be able to move as a unit with a common purpose toward a common goal.

Let's go a little further now in chapter 1.

Now I say this, that each of you says, "I am of Paul," or "I am of Apollos," or "I am of Cephas," or "I am of Christ."

> *Is Christ divided? Was Paul crucified for you? Or were*
> *you baptized in the name of Paul?* (vv. 12–13)

This is the second thing that keeps believers from walking in love. Your religion is carnal and vain as long as you are personality driven. The Corinthians were attracted more to personalities of the preachers than they were to the Word being preached. We're no different today. Some people won't go to church on Sunday unless the pastor is preaching. Friend, you can't be spiritual if you can only receive from a certain personality.

I think that sometimes we miss what God wants to do in our lives through the gifts that He sends to us because we become so attached to them as people that we don't let them flow in a realm of the Spirit. We see this so often among Christians in our nation. God raises up great ministers, and some people categorize themselves only by their favorite preacher. Now, we ought to know whom we are called to serve with. We ought to know where we are planted (and we should be planted in a local church if we want to grow). We ought to know whom God has given for covering over us. But if we want to really see God do something, then we have to get beyond just being attached to a person. If we get too attached to a personality, eventually we'll find ourselves following pastor so-and-so and not Jesus.

You can't be spiritual if you can only receive from a certain personality.

The church where I pastor is full of people with an abundance of gifts. But we can hinder the move of God if we get selfish with those gifts. If God opens a door and sends me to some nation or to some church for a few weeks to strengthen believers or to teach them something—things that I've been teaching at my church for fifteen years—and my congregation decides that they can't hear a sermon from anybody but me, then we've got a problem. If my congregation is so attached to me that it won't come to church and serve God because I'm not in the pulpit, then what kind of a charge would God lay to our account because of our selfishness?

Let's go a little further. There are some who, like the Corinthians, are too attached to style, skin color, or gender. There is something wrong with your heart if you can only hear speakers who have the same skin color that you have. There is something wrong if you can only hear men deliver the Word from God. There are some anointed women of God who have a life-changing word that you might miss if you're caught up like Corinth. In Christ Jesus, there is neither male nor female (Gal. 3:28). He puts His anointing in whomever He wants to use.

This is a mentality that must be broken. Some of you come to church to hear teachers, but you don't come to hear evangelistic gifts. Or you come and you love it when it's evangelistic, but you don't like to hear prophets. And some of you love to hear prophets, but you don't want to hear teaching. It is alright for you to understand what style influences you the most, to know what's easiest for you to receive. All of us have that. But some of the people who like teachers should hear some prophecy. If you only get teaching, you get puffed up, and prophecy has a way of shaking you up. If all you ever get is prophecy and never teaching, then you become flaky—all you see is a new day coming.

But if you never have teaching, then you can't recognize a false prophet. God didn't give just apostles. He didn't give just prophets. He didn't give just pastors. He didn't give just evangelists. He gave a fivefold ministry; he gave teachers, too.

Let's go on to 1 Corinthians 4:18–21. This is where Paul showed that he understood who is in charge.

Now some are puffed up, as though I were not coming to you. But I will come to you shortly, if the Lord wills, and I will know, not the word of those who are puffed up, but the power. For the kingdom of God is not in word but in power. What do you want? Shall I come to you with a rod, or in love and a spirit of gentleness?

Paul was having trouble with this church because he had sent Apollos and eventually Timothy to them to teach them. Not only did they start choosing sides, but some of them also rejected the teachers he sent and started preaching their own theology. They were running around with their own heresies, their own doctrines, and forming little clubs around their revelation. So Paul wrote and said, "I'm hearing that you all are trying to teach each other, and some of you are puffing yourselves up and thinking you can run this thing without the leadership I sent." Then he added, "Well, I'm going to find out when I show up whether you've got anything or not. If you do, you'll have some power in you. Oh, and when I come, you decide if I'm coming with a stick or if I'm coming in love." Sometimes people need to get a stick in the name of Jesus. That's what Paul said!

It is actually reported that there is sexual immorality among you, and such sexual immorality as is not even named among the Gentiles—that a man has his father's wife! (1 Cor. 5:1)

These Holy Spirit-filled people were speaking in tongues; jumping, hollering, and prophesying; having visions, dreams, and interpretations...and fornicating. Paul said it straight: *"And such sexual immorality as is not even named among the Gentiles."* In other words, Paul was saying that the church was doing things that the world wasn't even doing. There was a man who had been with his father's wife, meaning his stepmother.

For I indeed, as absent in body but present in spirit, have already judged (as though I were present) him who has so done this deed. In the name of our Lord Jesus Christ, when you are gathered together, along with my spirit, with the power of our Lord Jesus Christ, deliver such a one to Satan for the destruction of the flesh, that his spirit may be saved in the day of the Lord Jesus. (1 Cor. 5:3–5)

Paul didn't wait to get back to Corinth to deal with this one. He told them what needed to happen immediately. *"Deliver such a one to Satan for the destruction of the flesh, that his spirit may be saved in the day of the Lord Jesus."*

You are not spiritual when you are being led around in the flesh.

You are not spiritual when you are being led around in the flesh. Paul said that sexual immorality should not be named among us. There shouldn't be even a rumor of it. There are people who go to church who are easily moved by the Spirit of God, but also easily moved by their flesh. Paul said these people should not even be associated with.

Then he clarified his meaning by saying, "I'm not talking about those who are not saved." He said if that were the case, Christians would have to leave the world. No, he was talking about those in the church.

One reason the church does not have the power and authority it should is that even sinners know that some churches are filled with immorality. Now, that doesn't mean you're supposed to turn into the Holy Spirit Sheriff and run and try to get into everybody's business. It does mean, however, that when you see a brother or sister erring or doing wrong, you're supposed to go to that person and say, "Look, you've got to get this together. This is not the way you're supposed to be carrying on." I want to emphasize this because we live in a society that is defeated in this area. They are teaching our young people that they cannot be pure and be "normal." And unfortunately, the church, by its behavior, seems to be in agreement.

Society is telling our young people that they can't be pure and be "normal."

Flee sexual immorality (1 Cor. 6:18). If you are in relationship with someone and you transgress the law of God and keep on transgressing it, you need to get your heart right today. You need to go to that other person you are causing to sin too and say, "If we can't get this right, then today is going to have to be our last day of seeing each other or being in the same place together. I love you, but I love God more than you. And if we can't get this right, then we need to get away from each other."

Let's keep going in 1 Corinthians.

Dare any of you, having a matter against another, go to law before the unrighteous, and not before the saints? Do you not know that the saints will judge the world? And if the world will be judged by you, are you unworthy to judge the smallest matters?...I say this to your shame. Is it so, that there is not a wise man among you, not even one, who will be able to judge between his brethren? But brother goes to law against brother, and that before unbelievers! Now therefore, it is already an utter failure for you that you go to law one against one another. Why do you not rather take wrong? Why do you not rather let yourselves be cheated? (1 Cor. 6:1-2, 5-7)

If we saints are going to do business with each other, then let's do business properly. That means if you say you're going to do something, then do what you say you're going to do. And if somebody does what he says he is going to do, pay him—and pay fairly. Pay what you said you were going to pay him, without a check bouncing and without grumbling and complaining. Do what you said you were going to do. And if there is a conflict or a disagreement, don't feel that your first and only course of action is to sue somebody or take him to court.

God wants to bless His people even in the areas of business and prosperity. But sometimes we can't get that blessing because every time the saints start doing business together, this one is mad at that one, this one didn't do what he said, or this one thinks everybody else is trying to rip him off. The Bible says it's a terrible witness for you to be a Christian and take another Christian to court. God has given us all the tools we need to be reasonable with one another. Uncommon love requires patience, wisdom, long-suffering, understanding, and compassion. He also said it would be better for you to lose and somebody get one over on you than it would be for you to sue each other in the court system. That's not spiritual, that's carnal. And that's not love.

First Corinthians chapter 8 has to do with things offered unto idols.

> *We know that we all have knowledge. Knowledge puffs up, but love edifies. And if anyone thinks that he knows anything, he knows nothing yet as he ought to know. But if anyone loves God, this one is known by Him.*(vv. 1–3)

Here Paul was starting to talk about an area that has to do with liberty. This was a big deal among some of the Corinthians. When the pagans had religious ceremonies, they would sacrifice animals unto their gods. When the sacrifices and the religious thing were over, they would take that meat and go hang it up in the market to sell it. Some of the Christians were saying, "We won't eat that meat because it has been offered up to an idol." The other Christians said, "I'm hungry, and I'm eating the meat." These sanctified, spiritual, tongue-talking people got into a fight over who was holier—the ones eating the meat or the ones who wouldn't eat the meat. This fight got all the way back to Paul. Have you ever heard the saying of someone having "the patience of Job"? I think Paul must

Uncommon love requires patience, wisdom, longsuffering, understanding, and compassion.

have had an incredible amount of patience himself. He answered every disagreement.

> *Therefore concerning the eating of things offered to idols, we know that an idol is nothing in the world, and that there is no other God but one....But food does not commend us to God; for neither if we eat are we the better, nor if we do not eat are we the worse. But beware lest somehow this liberty of yours become a stumbling block to those who are weak.* (1 Cor. 8:4, 8–9)

What he basically said is that the mature understand that there is nothing unclean in and of itself. If you want to eat, eat. Their gods have no power over you. But there are other people who can't accept that. So to those people he said, don't eat. However, he continued, the one who doesn't eat it shouldn't think that he's more spiritual than the one who does. And the apostle admonished those who are stronger not to go forceing steaks on the weak.

Remember, these are the same people who are second to none in spiritual giftedness, and they can't get this thing straight. "What are we allowed to eat? What are we allowed to drink? Where are we allowed to go?" So he told them that those things are unimportant. His instruction applies to us as well. Don't get caught up in all those kinds of things. Stop majoring in the minors. Don't get all bent out of shape because your neighbor wants a Christmas tree in his house and you don't because it's a pagan symbol. If he's not worshipping the tree, what's the big deal? I plan on putting up a tree in my house, and I'm not going to be mad at you if you don't. You can call it Easter Sunday or Resurrection Sunday. Paul didn't care, and neither do I. I'm just glad that

Jesus got up out of that grave. Go ahead and carve your pumpkin and put it on your porch in October. I don't think that's going to keep you out of heaven. Actually, I think a lot of people are going to be surprised by who they see in heaven—and a lot are going to be surprised by who they don't see.

Next is chapter 9. Here Paul dealt with stinginess, which is more accurately described as a miserly heart.

> *Am I not an apostle? Am I not free? Have I not seen Jesus Christ our Lord? Are you not my work in the Lord?...Do we have no right to eat and drink? Do we have no right to take along a believing wife, as do the other apostles, the brothers of the Lord, and Cephas? Or is it only Barnabas and I who have no right to refrain from working? Who ever goes to war at his own expense?* (1 Cor. 9:1, 4–7)

Paul was saying, "Are you trying to say that I don't have the right to live by the ministry? That I don't have the right to eat and drink or take somebody with me to help me on my journeys like Peter and the rest of them?" He was telling them that they're being stingy. He noted that no one goes to war and has to buy his own gun or pay the bank note on the tank he's driving.

Paul was trying to do the work of God, planting churches, watching over the flock, writing to them, and correcting and encouraging them. But they wanted him to do all that and still make a living to support himself. He told them that they weren't spiritual, for if they were, they would understand that he shouldn't be out there at his own expense.

Are you seeing a pattern here? Every time Paul corrected them, he exhorted them to choose the way of love, and love always involves seeing to the need of someone else before you see to your own.

> *Therefore when you come together in one place, it is not to eat the Lord's Supper. For in eating, each one takes his own supper ahead of others; and one is hungry and another is drunk. What! Do you not have houses to eat and drink in? Or do you despise the church of God and shame those who have nothing? What shall I say to you? Shall I praise you in this? I do not praise you.*
> (1 Cor. 11:20–22)

They were class conscious. This was the problem. They were coming together to have the Lord's Supper, and everybody would bring his own. After the service, they would all eat together. The wealthy were bringing these large spreads with expensive wines. And they would sit there with all that food, and those who were poor were sitting next to them with hardly anything to eat. As you can guess, they weren't doing this for fellowship. They were doing it to show off their wealth. So Paul said, "I'm not going to praise you in this, when one can sit there with nothing while another sits next to him with his lavish spread. You're doing it to shame those who don't have anything."

Everybody comes to church the same way— under the blood of the Lord Jesus Christ.

The church is not supposed to be class conscious. That means when you come to church, everybody comes in the same way—under the blood of the Lord Jesus Christ.

Neither are the social inequities that exist in the world supposed to exist in the church. You don't get any points from God because you have a better job than somebody else who is struggling. You don't get any points with God because you own something that someone else doesn't. At the same time, you don't get any points from God by being broke either. It's simply all unimportant. Your status, your position in your community, externally, does not determine your position in the church.

I don't go out to lunch with people who have money and ask them to give a contribution to my church. If I've got to eat with you in order for you to have a heart of liberality, then the lunch is not even worth it. Please don't misunderstand; I think giving is holy. I think you should give as God prompts you in your heart. Bit if you've got to have personal attention in order to give, then that's manipulation and control. I don't let people control me. I'd rather not have the money and be free.

Your status in the community does not determine your position in the church.

Be careful. If you're around someone and God has blessed you with a lot more than he has been blessed with, don't exalt yourself in front of him. Don't try to make those people feel bad. Some of the very same people whom you are judging in your own heart and in your own mind, if you knew their story, you'd thank God that they are still standing. But since you don't know their story, it's easy for you to look at this little part and say, "Oh, that's off." If you knew their whole story, you might quit talking about them. You might say, "My God, you should get a star just for showing up."

Finally, if you read 1 Corinthians 12, you'll see that the Corinthians were carnal and without love because they were gift conscious. In other words, they measured a person's relationship with God by how he was able to perform spiritual things. Paul, however, told them thatGod has placed the members in the body as it has pleased Him. So if He gave us a gift, how can we brag about it? We didn't do anything to deserve it; God gave it to us.

Now we come to 1 Corinthians 13, of which Paul said, "Let me show you a better way."

The Better Way

Rather than worrying about people's gifts; worrying about people's personalities; having little arguments over who ate meat, who's got a pumpkin, and who's got a Christmas tree; rather than being sexually immoral and stingy and dividing yourselves up and creating heresies; Paul said, "Why don't you do this? Seek to walk in love. Seek to let love rule in your heart so that you can get along with each other and quit worrying about everybody else, and let Christ be exalted in your midst."

Love, Paul says, is the better way. First Corinthians 13 lists a few of the things that love is. But first, let's go to verse 11:

> *When I was a child, I spoke as a child, I understood as a child, I thought as a child; but when I became a man, I put away childish things.*

Maturity is related to love. Our growth in God should always bring us closer to Him and therefore closer to love.

Children tend to fight over things that don't really matter. Children make value judgments about things where there are no real judgments to be made. Who's better, Spiderman or Superman? Who sings better, Backstreet Boys or *NSYNC?

Maturity doesn't make a big deal out of the small stuff. It doesn't seek to separate people, but to bring them together. Maturity cares more for others than for self. Maturity is not prideful or envious. Maturity suffers long with people and is patient in circumstances. Is this starting to sound familiar? That's right. Maturity is love.

Look at 1 Corinthians 13 if you ever want to know if you have died to yourself and are living the life God has planned for you. Look at that passage and wherever you see the word *char ity* or *love*, replace it with your name. See how well you hold up. Are you patient, kind, meek, and forbearing? Do you hope all things, believe all things, and endure all things? Are you one who does not boast or seek your own good before someone else's?

If you will let Him, the Lord will be the death of you yet. He wants to kill off everything that doesn't look like Him. When He's finished, you will be walking, talking, testifying, joy-filled, peace-pursuing *love*. Your maturity in God will not be found in what you possess if you possess anything that He's not a part of.

Love takes pleasure in the flowering, or the prospering, of the truth. That's what love does. Love rejoices in the truth. And you will rejoice in the truth as it begins to flower and prosper in you. It's the uncommon life.

About the Author

About the Author

---◆ ◆ ◆ ◆---

Pastor Michael Pitts is pastor and founder of Cornerstone Church, located in Toledo, Ohio, and also overseer of a growing network of churches. Many church leaders regard him as one of this generation's most gifted leaders. His apostolic ministry is most noted for its spirit of excellence, divine order, and breakthrough anointing. As noted author and sought-after convention speaker, Pastor Michael Pitts has traveled extensively nationally and internationally.

Michael and his wife, Kathi, reside in the Toledo area with their two children, Meredith and Stephen Michael.

Journal

Journal Notes for Chapter One
Sacred Suicide

_____

_____

_____

_____

_____

_____

_____

_____

_____

_____

_____

_____

_____

_____

_____

_____

_____

Journal Notes for Chapter Two
This Is Your Wake-Up Call

_____

_____

_____

_____

_____

_____

_____

_____

_____

_____

_____

_____

_____

_____

_____

_____

_____

Journal Notes for Chapter Three
The Heart of the Matter

_____

_____

_____

_____

_____

_____

_____

_____

_____

_____

_____

_____

_____

_____

_____

_____

Journal Notes for Chapter Four
Matters of the Heart

_____

_____

_____

_____

_____

_____

_____

_____

_____

_____

_____

_____

_____

_____

_____

_____

_____

Journal Notes for Chapter Five
Show Me Your I.D

_____

_____

_____

_____

_____

_____

_____

_____

_____

_____

_____

_____

_____

_____

_____

_____

_____

Journal Notes for Chapter Six
What the Spirit Says

_____

_____

_____

_____

_____

_____

_____

_____

_____

_____

_____

_____

_____

_____

_____

_____

_____

Journal Notes for Chapter Seven
A Time for War

_____

_____

_____

_____

_____

_____

_____

_____

_____

_____

_____

_____

_____

_____

_____

_____

_____

_____

Journal Notes for Chapter Eight
A Time for Peace

_____

_____

_____

_____

_____

_____

_____

_____

_____

_____

_____

_____

_____

_____

_____

_____

_____

Journal Notes for Chapter Nine
Uncommon Love

_____

_____

_____

_____

_____

_____

_____

_____

_____

_____

_____

_____

_____

_____

_____

_____

_____

ANOTHER POWERFUL Book
from Whitaker House

All You Need Is a Good Brainwashing
Dr. Frank Summerfield

You are not a mistake. God strategically designed you with a purpose, a plan, and a destiny. Your mind is the key to unlocking your God-given destiny. Dr. Frank Summerfield exposes the tactics that the enemy uses to deceive you and challenges you to fight back by making the changes necessary to renew your mind to God's way of thinking. Discover who you were really created to be—victorious, successful, healthy, and full of purpose. Take the "scrubbing bubbles" of God's Word, open your mind, and give yourself a good brainwashing.

ISBN: 0-88368-771-2 • Trade • 192 pages

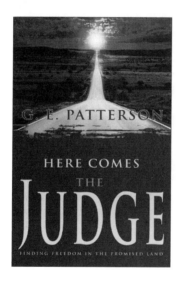

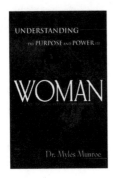
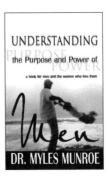
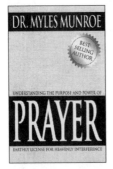